ABUSED CHILDREN

The Educator's Guide to Prevention and Intevention

Alan McEvoy, Ph.D.
Edsel Erickson, Ed.D.

L$_P$ LEARNING PUBLICATIONS, INC.
Holmes Beach, Florida

ISBN 1-55691-052-5

Learning Publications, Inc.
5351 Gulf Drive
P.O. Box 1338
Holmes Beach, FL 34218-1338

Printing: 5 4 3 2 1   Year: 8 7 6 5 4

Printed in the United States of America.

CONTENTS

PREFACE

Since our earlier book, *Child Abuse and Neglect,* our attention has expanded to include much more emphasis on how we as educators can help prevent child maltreatment from occurring in the first place. This is usually referred to as "primary prevention." Our role in basic prevention is broad. It involves educating all young people so that when they become parents they will respect the rights and integrity of their offspring. We believe that schools can do much in this regard — and do it in ways which are neither offensive nor costly.

Our role as educators is critical because no child protective services program will stop the increase in new child abusers. Only with the help of schools, in coordination with a variety of efforts in the social and economic sectors, can we hope to lessen the extent to which children are mistreated.

This book is also necessitated by new information about how the youthful survivors of maltreatment and their abusers should be helped, (i.e., secondary prevention or intervention). Educators need to know about what works and what makes matters worse.

In this book, our two main goals are clear. First, our schools must respond more effectively to the challenge of primary prevention in reducing the extent to which children grow up to become child abusers. Second, our schools must be more active and effective in assisting the community to identify abused children, and be capable in aiding in their survival and growth as good citizens.

Part A
The
Responsibilities
Of Educators

1
INVOLVING SCHOOLS

Since the 1970's, the mistreatment of children and adolescents has moved to the center stage of concern. The U.S. Congress and all fifty states have enacted legislation on the prevention and treatment of child abuse and neglect. The same is true in Canada. Hundreds of books and articles have been written on child maltreatment, including physical abuse and neglect, sexual exploitation, and psychological abuse.

Furthermore, child protective service agencies now constitute a vast bureaucratic network providing services to troubled families. There are a variety of national organizations addressing the problem, including the National Committee for the Prevention of Child Abuse, Parents Anonymous, Child Welfare League, American Humane Association, National Association for Children of Alcoholics, National Coalition Against Sexual Assault, and others. In other words, when compared to the 1970's, there has been considerable improvement in our attention to abused children and in our ability to respond.

It is also encouraging that our understanding of the maltreatment of children and adolescents is no longer viewed in isolation from other social problems. Child victimization has been linked to running away, suicide, substance abuse, bullying, spouse abuse, delinquency, adult crime, and a range of other social ills. Furthermore, our understanding of child abuse has moved away from simplistic psychopathological assumptions as a cause, to the complex interactions within the family and the environment.

Equally important, a range of treatments have emerged in recent years which show promise in assisting survivors of abuse and neglect. Included here are the services of not only mental health professionals, but law enforcement staff, agencies such as Girls and Boys Clubs, the YMCA and YWCA, religious organizations, and self-help groups composed of those who are survivors of maltreatment.

Finally, the issue of "victims rights" has entered the national political debate. The states and provinces have passed legislation which — to varying degrees — protects children when they are under the jurisdiction of the legal system. Simply stated, there has been progress on many fronts.

Despite this progress, however, the abuse and exploitation of our young has not ceased. Rather, it is growing as evidenced by the dramatic increase in the number of both physical and sexual abuse reports.

In addition, attempts to intervene in child abuse situations have generated new problems. For example, the courts and protective service agencies are often under fire for mishandling cases, for not responding to reports of abuse in a timely and effective manner, and for poor cooperation with schools and other organizations.

Some professionals are very cynical about the ability of Child Protective Services to address the problem. Accordingly, they do not always comply with reporting laws because, as one researcher notes, ". . . they see no benefits to clients. They point to low rates of substantiation and the failure of the state to provide funding for services to keep pace with the epidemic of reporting. They also suggest that the services provided are often ineffective" (Hutchison, 1993).

It is said that a "crisis management" ethic dominates society's response to the problem. By this it is meant that the bulk of effort is geared toward containing crises rather than preventing crises in the first place.

Whatever the merits of these criticisms, three generalizations can be made with respect to our success as a society in preventing child abuse. First, it is at the local level that prevention and intervention efforts will meet with success or failure. Second, the effectiveness of any community program to remedy child maltreatment is contingent upon the willingness of school personnel, medical and legal professionals, and human service workers to cooperate with one another. Finally, and most importantly, any comprehensive approach to the prevention and treatment of child abuse and neglect must involve the schools in more ways than in merely referring suspected abuse to protective services, or of being helpful to survivors of abuse. The school must be involved in primary prevention. Primary prevention means reducing the likelihood of child maltreatment in the first place by helping young people to grow into adulthood with the values, knowledge and skills which produce desirable parenting practices.

A high level of primary prevention is critical for two reasons. First, it is cost-effective, requiring no change in educational goals, and little shift in resource allocation. Second, because abuse is developmentally damaging to children and adolescents, primary prevention constitutes sound educational practice. This means that educators should have a primary interest in reducing abuse because it is a severe hindrance to the teaching of academic and social skills.

Yet, despite their vested interest, educators have not been as involved as they should be, especially given their knowledge, skills and access to young people. Often the actions of educators are limited to merely referring the growing number of abused and neglected children to authorities — and even in this role their actions are seriously restricted. For both valid and bad reasons, educators have overlooked many opportunities to reduce child abuse and neglect.

REASONS FOR
LIMITED INVOLVEMENT

Until recently, administrators, teachers and other school staff have been poorly informed about the nature and extent of child abuse and neglect. This is understandable. Most people were uninformed or misinformed about child maltreatment.

Evidence suggests that it was not until the 1960's that child abuse and neglect was "discovered" as a significant and widespread social problem. Prior to that time, child abuse commanded so little attention that even physicians encountering severely battered children failed to recognize the causes of the problem.

In addition, past failure to recognize and to report cases of abuse and neglect can be understood in the context of cultural assumptions surrounding parent-child relationships. Conventional wisdom suggests that it is "natural" for parents to love their children and to protect them from harm. It was inconceivable for most people — and it still is — to accept the idea that large numbers of parents would purposely hurt their children. Maltreatment of children violates the stereotype of benevolent parenthood.

Similarly, it is part of our culture that parents should physically punish their offspring. The old statement "Spare the rod and spoil the child" reflects a tradition which, from a cultural point of view, legitimatizes the physical punishment of children. Many also expect teachers to physically punish children when they misbehave. Moreover, court decisions supporting the use of corporal punishment in school have given legal sanction to the practice.

Even so, there is disagreement within and among legal, educational and other institutions over what constitutes proper punishment at school or home. What is considered "good discipline" from one perspective might be construed as "abuse" from another. As a consequence, a precise and generally acceptable definition of abuse by the culture at large, beyond that of "battering" children, is difficult to provide. Such cultural ambiguities contribute to the problem of identifying maltreatment.

There also is the commonly held value that educators should not interfere with the authority of parents. Many educators are understandably reluctant to involve themselves in child-rearing practices for fear of raising the ire of parents. They do not wish to be accused of usurping parental authority.

In the past, educators also feared that if they reported abuse or neglect, legal action might be instigated against them. Schools, like other organizations, are loath to become involved in litigation. Today, however, schools are protected from legal entanglements involving the "good faith" reporting of abuse and neglect. Nevertheless, past fears persist and act as deterrents to some educators who might otherwise intervene by reporting their suspicions of child abuse.

Furthermore, there are many who believe that a school's responsibility to a child should be limited to teaching basic skills and knowledge. Dealing with family problems or "risk diagnosis" is perceived by some educators as outside the realm of their professional duties and competencies. Ironically, many feel it is appropriate for school staff to report suspected cases of hyperkinesis, dyslexia, retardation, or other conditions which may contribute to learning problems, yet abdicate responsibility when it comes to child abuse and neglect which also affects learning. This truncated definition of school staff roles still contributes to a lack of appropriate school involvement in the reporting process.

Even in instances where some school personnel wish to report suspected cases, they may encounter problems with other staff who wish to protect the school's image, or possibly protect the parents from an intrusive investigation. This can be extremely detrimental to ameliorative efforts. Fortunately, however, schools have a legal mandate to protect staff who report suspected abuse and neglect cases, even if their superiors instruct them not to do so. Nevertheless, barriers to reporting child abuse persist.

The National Committee for Prevention of Child Abuse conducted a national survey of principals' attitudes and practices regarding child abuse. Principals were asked to cite reasons why educators may be reluctant to report suspected cases of child abuse. The results show that barriers to reporting continue to persist (see Figure 1.1).

FIGURE 1.1
BARRIERS TO REPORTING CHILD ABUSE

	Elementary Schools	High Schools
Fear of reprisal against child	60%	56%
Lack of faith in CPS intervention	59%	44%
Lack of knowledge regarding detection and reporting of abuse	44%	47%
Fear of parental reprisal	40%	22%
Interference in family privacy	39%	44%
Parental denial/disapproval	39%	25%
Legal ramifications for false allegations	34%	41%
Lack of community or school support	6%	6%

Source: Romano, Casey, L., and D. Daro. *Schools and Child Abuse: A National Survey of Principals' Attitudes, Beliefs, and Practices.* National Committee for Prevention of Child Abuse, Working Paper Number 851, July 1990.

Ironically, another reason for the lack of school staff involvement stems from the frustrations they experience when they do make a special effort to be helpful. For example, often when they report suspected cases of child abuse, they become frustrated at the responses of the protective service system. There are chronic complaints by educators about receiving little or no communication from child welfare and child protective service agencies. Frequently there is a lack of proper follow-up of reported cases. To outsiders there seems to be much mismanagement of legitimate cases of abuse, and endless delays in victims receiving assistance. The end result among many educators, whether earned or not, is a dangerous cynicism; they simply give up on trying to "make the system work."

To make matters worse, teachers, administrators and support staff often are uninformed about procedures for identifying, reporting and following up on abuse and neglect cases. Inservice training concerning the laws on child abuse and neglect, identification of symptoms of different types of maltreatment, specific procedures for reporting cases, as well as information concerning community agencies dealing with abuse and neglect, is inadequate or altogether absent in many school systems.

Moreover, many who are currently being prepared for teaching do not receive an adequate education on the topic of abuse. As long ago as 1977, the Education Commission of the States reported that the teacher education programs investigated spent an average of less than three hours instruction in understanding the nature, causes and consequences of child abuse and neglect. Even though much time has passed since these findings were reported, there has been little change in most teacher education programs. Unfortunately, the training "method" is usually "baptism by fire," where new teachers are thrown into abuse situations for which they are ill-prepared.

THE NEEDS OF EDUCATORS

With all the impediments that educators face, it is clear that our schools are nowhere near realizing their potential for lessening either the occurrence or the undesirable effects of child abuse and neglect. This is due in part to a lack of coordinated planning with community agencies. Educators need to understand how they can offer support services while still accomplishing their traditional academic goals. They are struggling to balance their academic responsibilities with the demand to solve serious social problems; and unless they can act more effectively, they will be unable to fully carry out either their social or their academic responsibilities.

There is little doubt, however, that educators are increasingly conscious of their role in reporting child maltreatment. In fact, in some parts of the country their referrals to child protective agencies are taxing resources to the breaking point. As this occurs, both child protective services and our schools are placed in the precarious position of having to wait days or weeks to act upon suspected cases which are filed.

Two obvious conclusions are warranted. The first is that more resources should be allocated to child protection agencies. The second is that further work needs to be done to foster more *effective* identification and reporting than has been the case to date. However, even if sufficient funds and trained staff can be found for child protection agencies, and even if every case of abuse and neglect is reported, there will still be the most important work for educators to do in reducing maltreatment — primary prevention.

REASONS FOR HOPE

Despite all the forces that impede educators, evidence suggests that school systems are increasingly recognizing their proper role to do more than merely refer children suspected of being abused. Educators are increasingly attuned to the fact that they must place greater emphasis on instruction in the knowledge, skills and attitudes that prevent youngsters from becoming abusers when they become parents. They are realizing more and more that they have both the right and the obligation to become involved. The child's right to protection by having parents who provide love and security without abuse is one of the primary prevention concerns of every socially conscious educator. Yet concern alone is not enough to solve the problem. Intelligent planning and action, based upon collaboration with the community, is required.

In the most profound sense, educators are the "frontline troops" in a societal effort to better the lot of our most vulnerable citizens. The actions of educators to help abused children, and to teach all students not to exploit others, will largely determine whether we are successful in becoming a more caring, humane and democratic society.

2
CLARIFYING OUR ROLE

It is one thing to assert that educators have a role to play in preventing child abuse, and it is another to describe that role. Here we must take into account laws, regulatory and enforcement agencies, customs, and the findings of researchers investigating child abuse and neglect. The first task is to consider recent child abuse and neglect legislation in the United States and Canada.

RECENT LEGAL TRENDS

Although there has been some protection of children from acts of extreme cruelty since the 1700's, the attention of legislators to child abuse and neglect is relatively new. Concomitant with the emergence of research in the early 1960's which documented the widespread existence of child abuse and neglect, a small group of physicians led by Dr. C. Henry Kempe persuaded the U.S. Children's Bureau to develop a law mandating that certain professionals must report cases of maltreatment (Besharov, 1985). By 1967 all 50 states had passed legislation explicitly requiring the reporting of child maltreatment to authorities (Davis and Schwartz, 1987). At the same time, similar laws to protect children were adopted in provinces throughout Canada.

Passage of the Federal Child Abuse Prevention and Treatment Act in 1974 provided funding for states to expand their child protection laws, and a flurry of legislation ensued (McEvoy, 1990; Hutchison, 1993).

The general thrust of this legislation was intended to serve several functions. First, these laws extended the categories of mandated reporters to include educators and other professionals. Second, these laws protected educators and other persons for "good faith reporting," affording them immunity from civil or criminal liability. Indeed, penalties were established for failure to report suspected cases of abuse or neglect. Third, these laws expanded the categories of behavior defined as abusive or harmful to children; they emphasized not only physical aggression and neglect, but sexual exploitation and the more general category of emotional or psychological abuse. Finally, these laws facilitated the development of child protective service agencies which receive reports, investigate cases, and determine appropriate intervention measures.

This legislation helped to create an infrastructure for child protection. As a consequence, the number of cases of abuse and neglect coming to the attention of authorities rose dramatically. For example, in the United States in 1972, an estimated 610,000 cases were reported to authorities. By 1982, according to the National Committee for Prevention of Child Abuse, more than 1.3 million reports were made, and in 1989 there were over 2.4 million reports. In the early 1990's, the number of reports each year is nearly three million. Because they are in a unique position to observe children over time, it is not surprising that a large percentage of these reports are initiated from educators.

The passage of hundreds of laws on child abuse and neglect in less than two decades is nothing short of remarkable. It is fair to say that the mission of child protection assumed an aura of near religious fervor in the 1970's. Legislators were eager to demonstrate that they were taking action to ameliorate a serious social problem. Even throughout the 1980's, both civil and criminal laws regarding child maltreatment expanded dramatically in Canada and the United States. There is little indication that this trend will abate in the foreseeable future.

The implications of this legislation for school policy and practice are profound. Most would agree that the protection of children is well-intended and reflective of deeply cherished values. Much of this legislation, however, poses great difficulties and challenges to educators as they attempt to comply with the letter and spirit of the law. From the onset of mandated reporting laws, a system of shared responsibility regarding authority over reports "...prevented the development of investigative expertise and encouraged administrative breakdowns" (Besharov, 1985: 151).

> **The problem for schools is that child abuse laws are often complicated, lacking clear definitions, devoid of administrative guidelines, and enacted in a fashion that mandates school action without the appropriation of adequate funding.**

Indeed, confusion still abounds as to the exact interpretation of most child abuse laws, as well as to how these laws should be translated into effective school policies. One reason for confusion is that the laws in any given state or province often do not coincide with the definitions of data collectors and practitioners in the field. Another is that many codes have not been tested in the courts.

To illustrate the problem, consider the concept of "injury." Child abuse laws show considerable agreement on the general *type* of injury (e.g., battering, molestation, serious untreated illness, etc.), but fail to clarify the *extent* of injury necessary for an act to be labeled abusive. At what point should corporal punishment be considered abuse? When do angry words translate into psychological injury? What constitutes serious neglect? Further compounding the problem, should standards of maltreatment which apply to small children apply equally to adolescents who are more mature? Other gray areas of the law are reflected in ambiguities in distinguishing between "reasonable" *vs.* "excessive" punishment of children, or "unintentional" neglect due to economic deprivation, *vs.* "intentional" neglect when parents are "financially able."

Given such ambiguities, there has been a tendency for both educators and child protection workers to direct their attention to the most palpable and extreme cases of abuse and neglect where injury is relatively easy to document. In other words, because the degree of harm necessary to trigger a report may be unclear, some undoubtedly respond only to the more obvious injuries. As a result, a large number of less obvious cases of abuse may not receive scrutiny.

Because of these ambiguities, there are continuous challenges in the courts to child abuse and neglect laws. The vagueness of terms such as "failure to thrive," or "serious harm," or "injurious to the child's health and welfare," have been alleged to be unconstitutional on the basis of being too broad.

We are now in a period of increased legal, professional and public concern over the perceived negative consequences of protection efforts (Besharov, 1987; Hutchison, 1993). In some cases, there have been highly intrusive investigations and other actions taken by protective service workers which violated the rights of parents, and which unfairly harmed the reputation of parents. Indeed, an organization called VOCAL (Victims Of Child Abuse Laws) has emerged to legally challenge the actions of educators, protective service workers, courts, and others mandated to carry out child abuse laws in the United States (Mayer, 1988).

Nevertheless, there is a continued trend toward more child abuse legislation. For example, states and provinces passed over four hundred pieces of abuse and neglect legislation impacting on schools and agencies in 1985 and 1986. Legal definitions of child sexual abuse have expanded to encompass prostitution and the production of pornography. New laws reflect concern not only with parents or guardians who are abusers, but also with abuse in institutional settings such as schools and day care facilities. Moreover, a number of states have mandated training programs for educators so as to improve identification and reporting. It is clear that definitions of abuse and regulations governing the conduct of professionals who deal with abuse situations have continued to expand (Davis and Schwartz, 1987; McEvoy, 1990).

This expansion of laws for the purposes of child protection poses a paradox. Broadly defined laws imply a broad responsibility to intervene, yet all-embracing definitions can result in actions which in turn are subject to procedural or other legal challenge. Obviously, the educator's responsibility is still in the process of evolving.

> **The paradox for educators is that the law expects them to act, without specifying precisely what their actions should be regarding child protection.**

Despite such ambiguities, two legal principles remain intact. First, mandated reporting laws which protect persons making reports are firmly entrenched and have not been declared unconstitutional. Second, the courts have generally accepted broad definitions of child abuse and neglect for the simple reason that it is impossible to specify every possible instance or condition of maltreatment. Court rulings tend to support the idea that broad definitions and subjective judgment can still facilitate the intended purpose of child protection by affording a measure of flexibility in the treatment of each case.

The variety of legal interpretations, however, has important implications for the schools. If concerted action in harmony with social and law enforcement agencies is required of our educators, then it seems that a great deal of shared understanding is essential. Furthermore, this shared understanding should be reflected in the working policies schools develop to deal with child maltreatment. At the very least, there should be some measure of agreement about the roles of educators. Certainly school and community leaders do not want to be working at cross-purposes. And they will not work together if they fail to understand and appreciate their mutual and differing responsibilities.

IMPORTANCE OF
PROTECTIVE SERVICES

Given the variety of views about child abuse and neglect, it is not always easy for educators to understand their obligations. To compound the problem, there are varying interpretations of child abuse among agencies charged with implementing laws.

It is also important to recognize that laws in regard to child abuse are expressions of intent by legislators. In a sense, we seldom deal with the law directly. Rather, we deal with those regulations that are supposedly designed to assist in the enforcement of law. Therefore, there is a need to be conscious of what these regulations are in our own particular districts, and how we as educators can best work together to implement them.

The regulatory agencies concerned with child protection services vary from region to region. Every educator should know the name of the child protective services agency in his or her school district. From them, educators should acquire the regulations and the laws for school involvement in child maltreatment cases, and be familiar with the protocol for handling reports.

As we have indicated, the regulations of child protective service agencies, like other regulatory bodies, are subject to emerging court decisions. But even so, the existing orders of regulatory agencies — including those of child protective services — usually carry the weight of law until changed by courts or legislative acts.

> **One conclusion is obvious: if we educators are to understand the operating definitions of child abuse and neglect, then we need to look closely at what the authorities in our districts are saying and doing.**

POLICY IMPLICATIONS

Because our laws are vague as to exactly what child abuse policy should be, educators may enact policies that still make them liable to the charge of not protecting children. Poorly defined policies can result in program gaps and inconsistencies in program implementation. This in turn may produce charges of school negligence and greater demands for accountability.

Given this situation, it is understandable that one driving force behind a school's child protection efforts often is a concern over possible liability. Thus, schools have two ongoing concerns: child protection and protection against liability. At times, these concerns are at odds with each other (McEvoy, 1990).

> **One method employed by many schools, which both enhances child protection efforts and appears to minimize the possibility of a charge of negligence, is the development of a team approach. Implied in reporting laws is a basic assumption: child protection requires the involvement of a number of persons and agencies in order to properly evaluate and respond to a child's needs.**

It is assumed that child welfare is best achieved through a multidisciplinary, coordinated approach. Consequently, teams of educators, mental health workers, social workers, nurses, law enforcement professionals and others often are formed for the purposes of sharing information, case review, and policy development. By enlarging the pool of expertise, the risk of making mistakes is minimized and liability is diffused.

In addition, many schools create policies which receive broad community support and thereby minimize the risk of liability. Such policies usually clarify the role of educators in the following areas:

- employment of child abuse and neglect teams;

- reporting of abuse and neglect;

- follow-up after a report has been made;

- contact with abusive parents;

- working with children who have been abused;

- working with protective services;

- incorporating primary prevention programming into
  the school curriculum;

- staff training and resource allocation.

Throughout this book, we will expand upon these roles
for educators. Suggestions will be made for developing
and implementing effective policies. However, we cannot
be expected to help maltreated children unless we first have
a clear sense of what we mean by child maltreatment.

WHAT IS CHILD MALTREATMENT?

There is no consensus on the one best definition of
child maltreatment. Nevertheless, three common ideas are
mentioned whenever child abuse is discussed. First, it
includes both acts of *omission* and *commission* by a parent
or guardian. Second, it encompasses a wide range of acts
that usually fall under one or more of the following
categories: physical abuse, sexual abuse, neglect, and
psychological abuse. Third, child abuse is not an
accidental act. The harm is intended.

While these three themes are important, it is this last
point — intended harm — which is somewhat confusing
but particularly relevant for understanding child
maltreatment. Does the harm need to be immediately
discernible when the abuse occurs, or can the damage occur
much later in the life of a child?

A Question Related to the Issue

In determining maltreatment, all too often there is a tendency to limit attention to those injuries which heal (e.g., broken bones and burns). Although such injuries deserve our concern, we believe that child maltreatment must also be understood in terms of harming the competencies in children — and in this latter case the damage may not be due to anyone's intentions.

What does it mean to impair the competencies of children? In answering this question, we are indebted to the contributions of James Garbarino and his associates (1980, 1982, 1986, 1991, 1992), as well as many other researchers. Their studies conclude that child abuse is developmentally damaging to children. Abuse can harm their physical, emotional or intellectual development.

As a consequence, maltreatment harms the abilities of children to competently perform various roles subsequent to the abuse. Abilities to relate to spouses, children, persons in authority, and others can be damaged as a result of being abused as a child. Intellectual development can be impaired by such divergent acts as malnutrition, beatings and repeatedly telling a child that he or she is stupid or unwanted.

Notice that in this view all harm need not be discernible at the time of the first injury. Further, the emphasis on competencies uses as a criterion of injury a body of research based on factors which can be objectively shown to impair functioning in later life, in the same sense as nutrition in childhood has been shown to affect cardiac functioning in adulthood.

The value of objectively examining child abuse and its effects is that it can then be understood transculturally (i.e., it is not limited to culturally relativistic definitions such as the variety of legal definitions of abuse that emerge). Child abuse as developmentally damaging to one's competencies should be ascertained regardless of local laws or customs. Heart diseases and its causes are not defined by laws or cultural norms, and neither should child abuse be determined by fiat, although laws should play one part of society's effort to reduce abuse.

From another perspective, the value of a view which takes into account both immediate and longer term consequences of abuse is that we are forced to consider the prerequisites for competent behavior, regardless of the specific role to be played (e.g., spouse, student, son or daughter, employee, citizen). Our analysis of the work of many researchers, therapists, educators and others leads us to conclude that there are four general categories of learned perceptions and feelings, and one skill, that are important forces in determining competency in almost any kind of human endeavor. They are perceptions in regard to safety, trust, power and self; and one's skill in communication.

Sense of Safety

There are certain minimum feelings of being safe that are an essential precondition for competent performance in any social role. For example, if a student knows that she will be abused by her father when she returns home from school, it becomes virtually impossible for her to concentrate on what is being required of her in the classroom. The child's anticipation that after school she will be unsafe is the focus of her concern, superseding all other considerations, including the demands of teachers for her to study.

> **When a child does not feel safe, when he or she lives under a constant cloud of threat, the ability to perform even routine tasks is undermined.**

Restated, the unpredictability and insecurity produced by anticipated abuse impairs the child in the development of competent role performance. Thus, even if the actual abuse never occurs, the threat of being harmed in one setting (e.g., home) can have harmful consequences in another area (e.g., school). And if there is one thing that occurs with child abuse, it is the perception of threat to one's safety.

Sense of Trust

Closely linked to feelings of safety are feelings of trust. The capacity to be trusting of others is essential for the development of competence in nearly every role that society offers. Trust is often a precondition for cooperation and sharing, and for honest and open communication. Trust is also critical to one's ability to nurture and to receive nurturance from others . . . to give and receive love. As humans, that which we most often value in our relations with others is predicated upon trust. Healthy relationships are trusting relationships. Healthy children tend to place their highest trust in their parents. If their parents violate their trust by being abusive, the children not only become distrustful of their parents, they come to distrust others, particularly persons in authority.

> **Abuse undermines the ability of children to develop positive, affective relations with others, including relations with those who are worthy of being trusted.**

Sense of Power

One consequence of believing in one's own competence is the ability to make decisions, to chart courses of action, and to have the confidence to carry out plans — even in the face of severe challenges. Believing in one's own competence in an area is to have a sense of power over events. A sense of competence causes people to believe they can make a difference. For example, self-conceptions of ability in mathematics (a specific sense of power) are associated with competent performances in mathematics classes. In fact, self-concept of academic ability has been shown in numerous students to account for more variation in school achievement than even cognitive ability *per se,* as measured by intelligence tests.

A common characteristic of children who are abused is that they come to feel powerless over their abilities to function normally in relations with others or in accomplishing certain tasks. Terrible things have happened to them — indeed, these terrible things may have been repeated over weeks, months, and years without anyone to help them. Not surprisingly, the ability of these children to make decisions, to act autonomously, to take command of their lives, or to be competent in many of the roles demanded of them is reduced.

Sense of Self-esteem

There is overwhelming evidence that levels of self-esteem in various roles affect the performance of people in their roles. When a child learns to feel unworthy or worthless, devalued, incapable, and thus deserving of abuse (low self-esteem), this can seriously undermine his or her abilities to perform both current and future roles such as spouse, daughter, son, employee, and so forth.

Child abuse tends to destroy feelings of self-esteem, producing instead feelings of guilt, estrangement, and self-loathing. These negative views of self in turn become self-fulfilling prophecies of repeated failures and minimal achievements. Low self-esteem that originates in maltreatment is debilitating to the development of many social, physical and intellectual competencies.

Communication Skill

Research evidence also indicates that child maltreatment is directly linked to the development of childrens' communication skills. Abused children often display serious limitations in the development of certain communication abilities. This is evidenced by problems ranging from withdrawal, attention deficits, and otherwise acting inappropriately. Problems in communication are compounded by the fact that these children may have been ordered not to talk — or simply feel unable to talk — to anyone about what they have experienced behind closed doors. Poor communication skills among such children also has been traced to social stigma — the tendency to be devalued in the eyes of others — that accompanies abuse.

In summary one's perceptions of safety, trust, power, and esteem, and one's ability to communicate effectively, combine to have a huge impact on competence in every area of human conduct. All of these important factors in child development are harmed by child abuse.

3
UNDERSTANDING ABUSIVE PARENTS

We know much more today than only a few decades ago about the causes of abuse. We know that child maltreatment is linked to many personal problems such as substance abuse and inappropriate learning. We also have some understanding of the social forces related to child abuse such as pressures in the market place, unemployment, job dislocation and homelessness. With this growing knowledge we are developing programs to assist educators, human service workers and others in their attempts to reduce the violence or neglect of parents.

Despite our growing awareness, however, it would be naive to assume that we completely understand abusive parents — and it is easy to uncritically accept myths about these parents, especially if one has had only limited experience and training in dealing with maltreatment.

MYTHS

It is false to assume that abused children are alike, or that their parents are all alike, or that they conform to a narrow range of characteristics. Examples of

misconceptions regarding abusive homes abound. Among
the most common myths are the following:

Myth:

If a person was abused at home, he or she will become
an abusive parent.

Fact:

Many parents who were abused as children do not
mistreat their own children. Moreover, many who were not
abused as children become abusers of their own offspring.
True, there is a statistically significant correlation between
being an abuse victim and becoming an abusive parent.
However, there are so many exceptions that we can easily
do great harm by automatically assuming that victims are
destined to be abusers. In fact most adults who were
victims do not abuse their children.

Myth:

Abusive parents hate their children.

Fact:

Most abusive parents believe that they are loving and
protective of their children. Most do not define their
children as "the enemy." Lacking parenting skills,
learning inappropriate parenting practices, or otherwise
feeling resentful about the demands of raising children is
not the same as "hating" one's offspring. In fact, most
abusive parents will do all they can to maintain custody if

they believe that the courts will remove their children from home.

Myth:

It is always best to remove abused children or abusive parents from their homes.

Fact:

There are clear instances where an abused child's interests are best served by removing the parent or the child from the home. In many cases such removal is helpful. However, removal dramatically alters family relationships, but not always for the better. The child's needs for an intact family should be assessed in relation to two conditions: the child's need for protection and the parent's willingness and ability to stop their abusive behavior.

Myth:

Criminal or civil penalties (e.g., jail or fines) are the best way of preventing parents from being abusive.

Fact:

Coercive measures are probably the least effective means of encouraging effective parenting. Such measures seldom prevent abuse and they are ineffective as a means of instruction in parenting. Criminal or civil penalties are an admission that society has already failed to prevent child abuse in the first place. Threat of punishments may deter *continued* child abuse in some instances, but overall it is not an effective form of prevention.

Myth:

Family violence is just a lower class problem.

Fact:

At first glance, there appears to be a disproportionate number of violent homes among the lower class. Poverty, single parenthood and other social ills are associated with abuse and neglect. In the general population, families on public assistance are four times more likely to be reported for child maltreatment. However, this observation should be tempered by several facts. First, there is a greater likelihood of detecting child maltreatment among lower class families because they are more likely to come under the scrutiny of professionals trained to look for abuse (e.g., social workers). Second, in middle and upper class homes where abuse is present, there are more resources to hide the abuse from others (e.g., able to afford going to various private physicians to take care of injuries). Finally, professionals know that all forms of child abuse (including sexual abuse) appear throughout the social class spectrum, and that most poor families do not mistreat their children. There is nothing inherent in a particular social class which dictates abuse, although the stress associated with poverty and limited social supports can increase the risk of child maltreatment.

Myth:

Parents who abuse their children are "sick" or mentally ill.

Fact:

The overwhelming majority of abusive parents exhibit no symptoms of mental illness. Probably no more than ten percent are psychotic or seriously neurotic. Thus, failure to learn how to be an effective parent is not evidence of a mental disorder. In fact, the belief that all abusive parents are "sick" only serves to further alienate them from the support they need to become better parents.

Myth:

All abused children have deep psychological problems; they are and will continue to be mentally unbalanced individuals throughout their lives.

Fact:

Without question, many survivors of child abuse carry psychological scars with them for life. Many need counseling and other supports. Surprisingly, however, most manage to get on with their lives and overcome many, if not most, of the negative effects of their abuse. When this occurs it is because of the appropriate support they received from friends, teachers, siblings, and others.

THE NEED FOR CAUTION

Given the danger of believing myths, it is crucial that when a child is suspected of being abused or neglected, a trained person visit and study the child and his or her home. It is for this reason that educators must have access to well-trained professionals from protective service agencies with whom they have developed a sound working relationship. These professionals should be in frequent communication with those educators who have made referrals about developments in each case.

In order to enhance understanding, inservice training in child abuse should be a regular feature of professional development in schools. However, one difficulty with employing lists which characterize abusive parents in these training sessions is that they usually lead to oversimplified and distorted views of the problem, what to look for and how to respond. The myths listed above can be reinforced in training sessions unless there is considerable elaboration and critique of the materials used.

ABUSIVE PARENTS

In exhibiting caution it is important that we not engage class or ethnic ethnocentrism in describing the more typical characteristics of abusive parents. To be sure, certain categories of abuse and neglect may be more easily observed in one social class than another. However, such observations should not be the basis of class bias. Child abuse is a pervasive phenomenon throughout our culture; it is not limited to racial, ethnic, or socioeconomic groupings.

Nonetheless, and with caution in mind not to reinforce stereotypes, we can say that abusive and neglectful parents as a group tend to share certain characteristics, such as:

- **They tend to be mistaught about parenting.** Often children model their parents. If their parents engaged in violence to raise them, then as adults they may do the same to their children, unless they learn elsewhere what is appropriate.

- **They often are socially immature** (especially if they are very young parents). The socially immature often lack coping skills to handle stress and many respond to stress with impulsive acts of physical or verbal aggression.

- **They tend to have low self-esteem.** One manifestation of this is a belief that their children are rejecting them.

- **They tend to lack even the most rudimentary understanding of the stages of a child's cognitive and physical development.** As a consequence, they often hold unrealistic behavioral expectations for their offspring, and they experience exaggerated frustration at the child's inability to meet those expectations. Often abused children are expected to be "small adults" capable of meeting their parents' needs, even though they lack such capabilities.

- **They often feel indifference or resentment toward the responsibilities of parenthood.** Some wish to be free of parenting demands; others invest little energy in planning to meet the physical and emotional needs of their children. For these parents, personal desires often take priority over the needs of their children.

- **Many abuse alcohol or other drugs.** In half or more of all cases of physical abuse, and in many cases of both sexual abuse and neglect, parental substance abuse is a factor.

- **Many physically abusive parents also have violent relationships with their spouses or live-in partners.** The character of intimate relations in the life of a child's parents has important implications for that child's risk of abuse.

- **Often they are socially isolated from a support network.** This impairs their functioning as parents during periods of intense stress.

- **Some belong to groups which require violence as part of child discipline.** For example, some religious cults practice violence against children (e.g., "spare the rod and harm the child" is taken literally). Others are members of families where a tradition of extreme punishment is considered normal and desirable.

Obviously, many of the above characteristics may or may not predispose parents to engage in abuse or neglect. We also should remember that parents with presumably similar characteristics often behave quite differently toward their offspring. Remember that in simply identifying the characteristics of abusive parents as a group, we have offered little insight into why any particular parent abuses his or her child.

It is also important to remember that while many teachers, counselors and other school staff eventually learn to identify physical and behavioral symptoms which are outcomes of abuse, they seldom see the *interaction* that takes place in abusive homes. In other words, it is difficult for most educators to fully understand what their students and their parents are like as they relate to one another.

Unfortunately, unless we educators understand what is happening between our abused children and their parents, we shall continue to be relegated to the role of crisis managers at best.

The critical point in understanding abuse is the way parents and children react toward one another, and not just what they are like independent of each other. If we are to understand and prevent child maltreatment, we need to examine the core of abusive relationships.

THE CORE OF ABUSE*

Most parents love their children and strive to protect them from harm. Yet under their own roofs, many parents engage in fundamentally destructive behaviors toward their offspring. The worst of these parents are untrustworthy, undependable, and abusive; they routinely rely on threat, intimidation or violence to get their way. They often are brilliant at manipulation, exploiting their children for their own ends, without due regard for the injuries they cause. In other words, they "use" the very people who need them the most and to whom they are most attached.

To be a "user" is to exploit others for selfish and harmful ends. A father who molests his daughter is misusing his power and position of trust. He is making her serve his felt interests without proper regard for her needs. In simple terms, he is selfishly causing her injury. This relationship between the incestuous father and his daughter

---

*This and the next section is adapted from _Youth and Exploitation: A Process Leading to Running Away, Violence, Substance Abuse and Suicide_ by Alan McEvoy and Edsel Erickson, by permission of Learning Publications, Inc., Holmes Beach, FL, 1990.

is characterized by an imbalance of power and a misuse of trust. The father's interest is in what the daughter can do for him, without consideration of the costs to her. She is treated by him as merely an object for serving his gratification.

The trauma for the victim is made even worse if the user implicates other loved ones in the abuse. An extreme example of this is a father who tells his adolescent daughter that if she doesn't engage in sex with him, he will have sex with her younger sister; or if she tells on him, the family will break up and her mother will no longer love her. The daughter is coerced to do what her father wants out of her concern for other people in her life.

Other cases of exploitation are not as obvious, yet are common. Consider, for example, the mother who subtly threatens to withhold her love unless her child does something that is only for the mother's benefit. The fear of rejection by one's parents is a strong force among children, even when they are teenagers. In fact, one of the typical ways that both young children and teenagers alike are intimidated is by a threatened loss of parental affection.

When parental love is dispensed conditionally, it creates in children insecurity rather than security, guilt and distrust rather than confidence and acceptance. In this sense, parental love is used as a technique of manipulation rather than being an end in itself.

Fear of rejection is a very potent force in the exploitation of children. When threats of rejection are coupled with other forms of exploitation, such as physical or sexual abuse, the consequences for the victim are both long-term and devastating.

A seeming contradiction exists in the relationships between exploitive parents and their children. Threats of being rejected are usually coupled with rewards. These rewards can be either unintended on the part of the offending parents, or they may be meant to serve as compensation for temporary feelings of remorse, or they may be intended to promote the continuation of exploitation. In the case of incest, for example, victims may be given gifts or other special favors. These rewards, however, can never compensate victims for the harm done to them.

> **At the heart of abusive relationships is a fundamental selfishness.**

Extremely abusive parents are so concerned with satisfying their own desires that they cannot or will not consider the interests, feelings or needs of their children. In other words, the preferences of exploitive parents dominate. During the period that abuse takes place, there is a serious absence of sympathy. Only after the abuse period is over does remorse sometimes occur. Remorse, however, is seldom sufficient to prevent the next verbal, physical, or sexual assault from coming, or to undo the damage. This is because abusive parents have tendencies that prevent them from recognizing in themselves their exploitive character.

> **Feeling sorry is insufficient to undo the damage caused by one's abuse of another.**

TENDENCIES TOWARD
EXPLOITATION

While there are unique features among abusive parents, nearly all exhibit similar ways of interacting with their offspring. Abusive parents tend to:

- **deny** responsibility for their abusive actions;

- **blame** their victims for the abuse;

- exhibit **hypocrisy** in that they "preach" one thing but do another;

- inappropriately **dominate** their children;

- **mistrust** their victims and those who might get close to their victims;

- **violate** the basic rights of their children;

- present **contradictory messages** of "you are damned if you do and damned if you don't;" and

- **compulsively repeat** their abusive behaviors.

Denial

A common characteristic of abusive people is their failure to recognize or to admit that their behavior is abusive. It is as if they are "wearing blinders," particularly at the time they are abusive. No parent wants to admit responsibility for harming his or her child. Even in the face of considerable evidence that their actions are injurious, most abusive parents will deny their abuse, or minimize the negative consequences of their actions.

> **One reason for denial is that exploitive parents often care about their children, even though they abuse them.**

It is extremely painful to admit that one is abusive. To avoid such an admission is a way of avoiding feelings of guilt and depression. Even when abusive parents are directly responsible for their children committing suicide, running away or abusing drugs, they will deny their role as a way of reducing their pain. Abusive parents nearly always find a host of excuses to absolve themselves from confronting the truth of their misconduct.

> **Another reason for parental denial is that by admitting responsibility for being abusive, a psychological pressure is created to behave differently toward their children.**

Abusive parents who admit to being abusive feel intense pressure to change habits upon which they have come to rely. Much like an addiction, abusive parents become so attached to certain ways of interacting with their children (e.g., becoming verbally or physically violent in the context of "discipline") that it is hard for them to believe that change is possible or desirable. *Denying the harm of their conduct relieves them from the prospect of having to alter how they act.*

> **Many abusive parents convince themselves that the real harm comes not from continuing a set of injurious actions toward their children, but rather from *changing* their behaviors.**

A parent who uses excessive verbal chastisement or physical violence to "motivate" a child usually believes that no other method of discipline will work. To use less extreme or different forms of control is viewed as counterproductive. For such parents, emotional or physical violence is rationalized as beneficial to their children rather than as injurious. Parental statements such as "I'm doing it for your own good," or "This will make a man out of you," illustrate such rationalizations. These rationalizations are a way of denying harm and of feeling justified for having been abusive.

Yet even when parents admit to having inflicted harm, they can still engage in denial. They may not deny the harm they caused, but rather they deny their *intentions* to harm. For example, getting drunk is often a necessary preliminary for an incestuous father to sexually abuse his child. Even though he realizes the harm done, the drunkenness becomes a convenient excuse to save face and to deny that he is "that kind of person." Such denials allow parents to use their children and yet be convinced that it happened because of circumstances "beyond their control." Consider how often abusers will try to explain their actions with a phrase such as "I'm not really like that . . . I only did it because I was drunk."

> By employing such excuses as "I was drunk, that's not really me," the abuser thus creates a psychological basis for continued exploitation.

Denial by an abusive parent is also a means of manipulating the perceptions of others outside the family. If the denials are believed by others, then the parent is cast in a more favorable light.

> The end result of these denials is to allow the exploitation to continue for months or years without others intervening.

Blaming Victims

It is seemingly easy for exploitive parents to point the finger of blame at their children. For example, a stepfather who sexually molests his ten-year-old step-daughter may claim that she was being "seductive" or had subtly invited his "special attention." Another example is the violent parent who states that "It's your fault for making me so angry," or an alcoholic parent who blames the child for causing him or her to drink. By blaming the child, the offending parent shifts the attention of both the child and others away from his or her abusive behavior. Blaming the victim also allows exploitive parents to deny responsibility for their actions. Taken together, denial and blame are the fuel of abusive relationships.

Hypocrisy

Another pattern among exploitive parents is to engage in hypocritical behaviors relevant to the abuse. The mentality is one of "Do as I say, not as I do." An alcoholic parent who dwells on the dangers of drinking, or a sexually abusive parent who "preaches" about the immorality of intimate relationships, fits into this category. In a fundamental sense, exploitive parents serve as hypocritical role models. Their actions are in direct opposition to the ideal values they claim, as well as to those of society. Sadly, few abusers ever see the contradictions in their behavior.

Ironically, many view themselves as paragons of morality, pointing the finger elsewhere for the harm that they cause.

Domination

It is also common for abusive parents — particularly those who are violent — to demand unyielding submission to their authority. They are excessively domineering. An abuser's "authority" allows for no challenge. Even the most unreasonable requests take on the aura of a commandment. When a child or teenager fails to submit to such parental domination, the abusing parent often responds with extreme anger and overly severe punishment. This "righteous anger" in turn reinforces a tendency to blame the victim for the abuse.

> The mentality of exploitive parents is one where
> their children are expected, indeed commanded, to
> do exactly as told, even down to the minutest
> detail.

Mistrust

Another characteristic of exploitive parents is a basic
mistrust of their children. This mistrust is particularly
evident when their children are outside of their immediate
control (e.g., on dates, at school, with friends). Such
mistrust is a direct result of the exploitive parents' desire to
maintain a shroud of secrecy. Any event or interaction
which might reveal the abuse to "outsiders" is suspect.

Not only is the victim mistrusted by exploitive parents,
but so too are the victim's friends or relatives who are in a
position to learn the truth. As a result, the offending parent
often attempts to isolate the child from others, especially if
there is a perceived risk of discovery. This is similar to
spouse abuse. An abuser simply cannot afford to risk
others learning about his or her child's predicament.

> By attempting to isolate his or her child, the
> abusive parent seeks to avoid detection and to be
> able to perpetuate the abuse.

Violations of Rights

Abusive parents regularly intrude in a highly
exaggerated manner on the freedoms of their children, and
sometimes their children's peers as well. Frequent

interrogations of peers and other family members concerning the actions of their children, invasions of privacy, and a denial of basic human rights are common. Again, these intrusions are designed to maintain control over their children and to keep any abuse secret. A typical example of such intrusive surveillance is the sexually abusive father who monitors virtually all of his daughter's activities, and jealously interrogates her dating partners and friends about her outside associations. Other examples include opening their children's mail and spying on them.

> **Violations of rights are one of the chief mechanisms by which exploitive parents keep their offspring isolated from those who might otherwise be in a position to intervene.**

"Damned If You Do, Damned If You Don't"

Regardless of what some abused children do, it is either wrong or not good enough. In essence, many abusive parents impose a "no win" situation on their offspring. The inevitable failure of the child in the context of this no win situation becomes in turn, further justification for harsh treatment.

> **Abused children and teenagers often are put in the position of being unable to satisfy the abusive parent, no matter how hard they try.**

Educators should be alert to this phenomenon. For example, certain students may be able to improve their grades from F to A, and still not satisfy their parents. In such cases, the parents simply ignore or underplay this accomplishment and focus instead on some other perceived failure of their offspring.

Compulsive Repetition of Abusive Acts

One of the most harmful dimensions of an exploitive parent's relationship with his or her child is when abusive behavior is compulsively repeated. Whatever kind of abuse the exploitive parent engages in, it often takes on a ritualistic aspect. By "ritualistic" it is meant that there is a sequence of events before, during and after the abusive episode, which are repeated over and over again. While the sequence will vary from person to person, each abuser tends to follow a pattern (e.g., getting drunk, picking a fight, becoming violent, and then acting as if nothing ever happened).

Only rarely is victimization ended by the victim being able to mobilize sufficient resources to finally make an escape. The longer the abuse continues, the greater the likelihood that victims will experience long-term trauma. Also, the longer the abuse continues, the more difficult it is for victims to extricate themselves.

> Once a pattern of abuse is established, the frequency and the intensity of the abuse tends to escalate. **Without deliberate outside intervention or the incapacitation of the offender, there is little likelihood that the abuse will abate.**

It is probably true that most relationships between parents and their children, including healthy parent-child relationships, will at times involve some selfishness. Yet there are several key considerations which distinguish abusive parents from healthy parents. With exploitive parents, the abuse occurs frequently, is severe in intensity, and it continues for long periods of time, even years. Moreover, the harm done to their offspring is often conscious and intentional, despite denials to the contrary. Even in light of having caused obvious injury (e.g., a severely battered teenager), these parents tend not to change how they behave toward their children.

> Among healthy parents, there is the satisfaction of knowing that they have tried to help their children. For children of emotionally healthy parents, the benefits are feelings of security, trust, and the ability to share their feelings with others. These children, like their parents, learn how to love and to be loved by others.

4
A PROFILE OF
ABUSE SURVIVORS

When children and adolescents are abused, how do they learn to perceive the world about them? What do they learn about themselves and about the character of intimate family relationships? How do they learn to cope when they are being exploited by the very persons who should act as loving protectors?

It is common among survivors of physical or sexual abuse to have feelings of fear, distrust, rejection, low self-esteem, and a pervasive sense of powerlessness. These children may learn to isolate themselves from others as a means of avoiding conflicts. They may have learned that it is best not to trust anyone, and hence do not seek assistance for themselves. They may have been ordered by parents never to talk to anyone about what goes on at home. Many of these victims have never learned to develop healthy and nurturing relationships with others. In short, many of the competencies one might take for granted in others, are underdeveloped or absent in these children. When encountering abused children and teenagers, educators should learn to recognize the following characteristics.

Attachment to Parent(s)

Most victims have deep attachments to their parents, although they may resent how their parents are treating them. Victims — especially when they are young — also continue to be in a dependency situation with their parents. This means that the parents usually continue to meet some of the basic needs of the child (e.g., food, clothing, shelter) even while the child is being abused. Such dependency fosters attachments which are not easily broken, even when they are accompanied by exploitation. In other words, do not expect victims of parental exploitation to automatically hate their abusive parents.

Self Blame

Because abusive parents often are experts at denial, anticipate that children who exhibit symptoms of abuse or neglect may not define themselves as victims. Many victims of prolonged maltreatment believe that their home situation is normal and hence they do not fully recognize what is happening to them. Oftentimes they feel profoundly guilty and claim that it is they, rather than their abusing parents, who are responsible for what has happened as reflected in comments such as "I made him so mad that he had to hit me." They may also believe that their parents have a right to treat them a certain way. There is sad irony when victims fail to recognize that they are being exploited in that they are unlikely to seek help, and thus they are left in the unfortunate position of being abused over and over again.

> Many abused children learn to accept their
> abusive parents' view of events, and believe that
> they caused their parents to harm them.

Denial

Abused children are very fearful of "causing" their families to break-up, or of their parents going to jail. They tend to deny being abused out of loyalty, and out of fear of being responsible for causing their families trouble. They are also likely to continue to protect their abusing parents for another basic reason: the prospect of having to move into foster homes is often more frightening than staying in a familiar albeit abusive environment. Thus, you should anticipate that maltreated children and adolescents will want to protect their parents by denying what is happening to them.

Mistrust

Being harmed by a parent constitutes a "core experience" wherein fear, distrust and withdrawal are a means of coping with a fundamental contradiction: their protectors are harming them. As such, they may believe that no one can be trusted, including those who seek to help them.

Such feelings of mistrust are easily generalized to nearly all relationships when the child feels unsafe at home. Feeling safe is a basic prerequisite for competent functioning in almost any situation. And when abused children and teenagers learn that their home is not a safe haven, it is difficult for them to believe that they can be trusting in other settings. Sadly, once a victim develops a deep mistrust of others, almost any relationship which might hold the potential of becoming emotionally intimate triggers a response of rejection. As a result, many victims suffer for years, isolated from meaningful and loving relationships, because they have mistakenly learned that trusting others makes them vulnerable to exploitation.

> **Expect that victims of parental abuse will have a difficult time trusting all adults.**

Powerlessness

The ability to perform competently in one's social roles has as its foundation the belief that one has a measure of control over his or her life. In other words, the premise that one has the power to make and to carry out decisions — that one has the ability to act upon the world and not merely be acted upon — is essential for competent role performance. When children are raised in an environment of abuse, their sense of personal power is fundamentally undermined; they feel that their lives are dictated by others because they can neither prevent nor escape being abused.

The result of feeling powerless is low self-esteem, indecisiveness, fatalism, a tendency to act out in inappropriate ways, and unfortunately, an increased probability that survivors will be so lacking in self-confidence that they enter into unhealthy dependency relationships with more assertive peers or adults who, in turn, further exploit them.

It is certain that to weaken young peoples' feelings of power and self-esteem because of abuse is to dramatically risk their ability to function as competent and healthy citizens.

Isolation and Moral Confusion

Accompanying feelings of mistrust, low self-esteem, guilt, and powerlessness among many victims are two other related feelings: a profound sense of isolation, and deep feelings of moral confusion. The isolation is partly a result of the abuser intentionally manipulating the social environment of the abused in order to reduce the likelihood of discovery, and partly the result of the difficulty the victim has in learning how to establish healthy and trusting relationships with others.

Given these conditions, it is not surprising that many victims believe that they are "alone in the world." This isolation is made worse by the fact that the abuser constitutes a powerful role model for the victim. Abusive behaviors are made to seem legitimate and normal by the abuser, especially in order to achieve what one desires. Certainly such messages about human relationships are a source of great moral confusion because they stand in direct opposition to what most healthy people believe to be acceptable.

Little wonder that when such exploitive behaviors are carried out with impunity by a child's role models, the child often learns to imitate these destructive actions. In turn, such behaviors can drive others away who might otherwise be supportive, thus reinforcing the victim's sense of isolation.

Limited Communication

For many young people, one consequence of prolonged abuse is an impairment in a willingness or ability to communicate on an affective level. Maltreated children simply are unable to express to others how they feel, perhaps in part because they have not been *allowed* to talk freely about their experiences at home. As they grow older, they also become sensitive to the stigma associated with being involved in an abusive relationship. They hold their hurt inside and "put up a front." They do not believe that others could possibly understand what they have experienced. Thus, there is little likelihood of their asking for help or of accepting help, even if it is available.

This means that it is a mistake for anyone to expect or to encourage abused children to feel a debt of gratitude for help they may receive. Many abused children have such limited communication skills that they do not know how to express thanks when help is offered. Furthermore, feelings of indebtedness can turn to resentment if the help giver demands recognition for the help given.

> **Many students in need, especially teenagers, will refuse assistance in order to avoid feeling indebted.**

Even if abused children and adolescents do receive help, educators should not expect any "miracle cures." Victims of abuse often have experienced a pattern of maltreatment extending over months or years. As such, these children may have developed coping strategies which are troubling to school personnel (e.g., lying, acting out, withdrawal). This means that educators should not be discouraged if their efforts to help abused students do not meet with immediate success.

While educators should be aware of the patterns commonly associated with being victimized, they should never assume that all abused children are the same or that they have identical needs. No single approach is applicable to all. Certainly the relationship between educators and abused children should develop naturally without seeming contrived or forced.

> **Being patient, empathic, and honest with abused children nearly always is a precondition for successful intervention.**

The "Stockholm Syndrome"

One of the questions that perplexes many people is: Why do so many abused children and teenagers continue to endure incest and other severe parental abuse without resisting or escaping? This question is not unlike the question: Why do so many battered wives stay with their abusive husbands? One answer to both questions is to be found in understanding the "Stockholm Syndrome."

The term "Stockholm Syndrome" was coined in the wake of a Swedish bank robbery where people were held hostage and terrorized for six days. What happened was that some of the hostages developed feelings of gratefulness, alliance, and even affection toward those who terrorized them. It is as if the victims were wearing blinders in that they overlooked the bad things done to them and instead, focused on apologies for their terrorists. This phenomenon occurs not only in terrorist-hostage situations, but also in more intimate relationships where parents abuse their children and husbands abuse their wives.

There are five conditions which form the basis of the Stockholm Syndrome:

1. The terrorist is seen by the victim as one who poses a severe threat to the victim's very survival.

2. The victim feels unable to escape from the terrorist.

3. The victim feels psychologically isolated from others who could be of assistance.

4. The terrorist manipulates the situation such that the victim is helpless and comes to be dependent on him or her to meet basic needs.

5. The terrorist displays a measure of "kindness" towards the victim, often in the context of meeting the victim's dependency needs.

This final condition — a display of "kindness" — is especially critical for it encourages the victim to deny the abuse and "bonds" the victim to the abuser. This dual process of denial and bonding is a means by which the victim can cope with a situation over which he or she has no control.

Such "kindness" reinforces the victim's belief that the exploiter is "not really so bad," or that the perpetrator will "change." This helps to explain why some victims, even in the aftermath of horrendous exploitation, do not display anger toward their abusers. It also explains why many victims of exploitation do not leave the situation or report the abuse. Hence, what seems like self-destructive behavior from the outside is really a survival mechanism: the victim is in an untenable situation, responding reasonably to an unreasonable set of conditions which have been imposed upon him or her.

The term "syndrome" does not mean that the victim is responding in an abnormal manner. Rather, it is an understandable reaction given the conditions of terror, isolation, extreme dependency, and "kindness." It is also noteworthy that victimizers usually are very deliberate in creating these conditions. Abusers know how to manipulate in a way that increases their chances to continue exploiting while decreasing the risk of discovery.

> **The survival reactions of many victims, unfortunately, serve to reinforce the victimizer's exploitive behavior.**

The "Oh Woe is Me" Syndrome

There is one final characteristic that is common to victims which is both perplexing and tragic. This characteristic encompasses the feelings of insecurity, distrust, powerlessness and isolation already discussed. However, this characteristic appears, on the surface, to be the opposite of denial. It is what we refer to as the "Oh woe is me" syndrome. It is when victims of exploitation learn to see themselves as victims and then use this identity to manipulate others.

The "Oh woe is me" syndrome represents a *strategy* that some exploited people learn in order to help them cope with a terrible set of circumstances in their lives. When one has been a victim for a long period of time, it becomes increasingly difficult to deny to self and to others the harm that is done. Initially there may be denial. Yet attempts to deny repeated abuse become less convincing over time and do not alter the basic conditions of the abuse. For many victims, there is a gradual realization that denying their hurt and confusion has not helped them. It is at this point that they may learn that admission of harm can be used as a tactic to gain some advantage.

The consequences are several. First, victims become so "fixated" with their having been victimized that in some respects their emotional growth and maturation is arrested. The abuse they endured seems to be a major focus for them in that it is frequently referred to on a daily basis. They may regularly bring it up in conversations, even when the topic of discussion appears to be unrelated. Even when others are "sick and tired" of hearing about it, some victims seem unable to refrain from making reference to their having been victimized.

> **Some victims of exploitation use what has happened to them as a tool to elicit attention, pity, or even special favors from others. They may also use what has befallen them as a convenient rationalization for their own inappropriate conduct toward others.**

Even well into adulthood, long after abuse survivors have ceased to be harmed, the trauma of an earlier time is used as a justification for their actions. For some, it is a handy excuse for failing to change habits over which they do have control, such as being abusive parents or spouses.

Second, a related consequence of obsession with being a victim is that it drives potentially supportive people away, thus making an abused person feel even more isolated and powerless. There comes a point in most relationships where others are no longer willing to accept an abused person's victimization as an excuse for undesirable conduct. There is a feeling that the victim must take control of his or her life and no longer be defeated by events that happened in the past. There is also a sense of resentment when a victim continually uses being harmed as a means of gaining sympathy or attention. While taking advantage of people's sympathy for them may *temporarily* help victims to cope, in the long run it only adds to their trauma.

> **The inevitable outcome is that those close to the victim begin to feel resentment rather than empathy. Their sympathy turns to anger and disgust. Indeed, they may even begin to withdraw, thus reinforcing the victim's feelings of distrust, isolation and lack of worth.**

IMPLICATIONS FOR EDUCATORS

By studying the lives of abused children and teenagers, educators can draw two basic conclusions. First, the undesirable emotional and behavioral problems of victims of abuse emerge as *consequences* of their being victimized and are not the causes. Many educators mistakenly believe that the misbehavior of students who are abuse victims is what caused them to be harmed by others. The responsibility for being abused is misplaced on students for problems which were, in the first place, caused by their having been harmed.

Second, it is a mistake to assume that all abused students will become impaired adults. Some, if circumstances are favorable, will go into adulthood as relatively healthy individuals. Others will be hurt so badly that their mere survival is an accomplishment. It all depends upon what else happens to them, including what happens in school.

This means that a high priority should be given to teaching teachers and other school staff how to identify signs of maltreatment and how to help those who are victims.

IDENTIFYING SIGNS
OF MALTREATMENT

Teachers are often among the only adults standing between maltreated children and the parents who harm them. But to help abused children they must first recognize the indicators of abuse. What can teachers and others use to make such as assessment? How useful are lists of warning signs?

The most important point here is that lists of abuse and neglect warning signs should only be used to sensitize educators to the *possibility* of maltreatment. Only a thorough investigation by a trained person will allow for a reasonably valid determination of harm. Nonetheless, because children have more contact with school staff than with most groups of adults outside the immediate family, it is crucial that staff members be aware of these signs.

WHEN OBSERVING STUDENTS

While there are many correlates of maltreatment, some children who are **not** mistreated will also exhibit them. There are also students who do not exhibit any obvious signs, yet they too can be victims of parental abuse. Because the appearance or actions of maltreated children may or may not indicate abuse, caution is in order; no conclusions should be drawn about a possible case of abuse or neglect until it has been investigated by trained persons who are legally mandated to conduct such investigations. Nevertheless, there are common behavioral warning signs displayed by children which indicate possible parental mistreatment.

Behavioral Signs of Maltreatment

Parental maltreatment can produce any number of behavioral responses in children. Figure 4.1 lists those that are commonly observed in cases of child abuse and neglect. However, a quick review of this list also should suggest that some signs of maltreament are similar to those of disabilities that are produced by harmful forces other than abusive parents. Any number of events can hurt the development of children. Thus, one should be cautious when these signs are observed. Look at the total context, and seek confirmation from professionals.

Figure 4.1
Possible Behavioral Signs of Abuse

Hostile to authority • excessively disruptive • overly aggressive or destructive •
rapid drop in school performance • excessive lying or cheating • extremely passive
or withdrawn, shrinks from physical contact • excessive crying with little apparent
reason • fearful in the presence of parents or other adults • easily distracted, bored
with normally stimulating activities • listless with no apparent reason • suddenly
develops a speech problem • exhibits manic depressive extremes, phobias •
habitually tardy or absent • abrupt illness on days when scheduled for physical
education • complains that physical activity causes pain • loiters outside of school
after the school is out • always hungry • eats only junk food • regularly eats food
that is left on classmates' trays • steals lunches • confides sexual experiences with
adults or family members • is overly sexually active • talks of low self-worth, being
damaged, acts depressed • runs away • attempts suicide.

We wish to stress again that many of the behaviors
listed in Figure 4.1 characterize students who are not
abused. Consider, for example, so-called "acting out"
behaviors. These behaviors may be the child's way of
asking for help, or they may reflect what the child has
learned at home. Perhaps modeling one or both parents, the
child expresses what he or she has experienced. If the child
has experienced violence at home, he or she may tend
toward being violent at school. But students also act out
due to peer pressures or for other reasons. It is
inappropriate to automatically jump to the conclusion that
misbehavior is due to abuse at home. Thus, be cautious in
drawing conclusions; always consider the total context
within which each observed behavior occurs, and depend
upon a trained child protective services worker for
confirmation.

In addition, when confronted with an aggressive or
belligerent student, educators may find it difficult — some
may find it impossible — not to strike back either
physically or verbally. Yet if educators are to help children

shed these unacceptable behaviors, they must adopt positive responses.

> **Seeing the abused child as a "survivor" rather than as an "incorrigible" is a reasonable first step.**

Educators are often so busy trying to cope with aggressive or uncooperative children that they ignore those who are quiet and withdrawn. Indeed, it is not uncommon to find teachers identifying such children as "model" students. A child who exhibits withdrawing behaviors also might be in serious psychological trouble. Educators should be as concerned about this type of child as they are about the physically aggressive or unruly child. They should refer the child to the school psychologist, social worker or counselor if he or she appears to be withdrawn, isolated or unable to establish personal relationships with classmates.

When a student is consistently observed "hanging around" before and after classes, one may suspect that something is wrong at home. Such behavior can reflect a home situation characterized by lack of parental supervision, indifference, and possibly abuse. In cases where a student consistently hangs around school, the staff should plan a conference with the parents to discuss their child's actions. If the situation suggests abuse or neglect, a referral should be made.

The most critical behavior requiring immediate attention involves a youth threatening or attempting suicide. It is not the responsibility of the educator to determine whether such behaviors are intended merely to "get a reaction," or are a serious attempt at self-destruction. Whatever the reasons for suicidal behavior, educators should immediately refer the student to experienced professionals.

Other Signs of Physical Maltreatment

Not only should educators look for behavioral indicators of maltreatment, they should also learn to recognize the physical signs. School staff can learn a great deal about a student's home situation by being sensitive to his or her physical appearance. School staff should be especially alert when they observe a pattern of the signs listed in Figure 4.2.

Figure 4-2
Possible Signs of Physical Abuse

There is a history of repeated injury • appears regularly at school wearing inappropriate dress for the weather conditions (e.g., clothing is not adequate for protection against the elements; or wears long sleeves regardless of how warm it is inside or outside the building) • often has bruises on the arms or legs, black eyes or welts • has burns on the arms, legs or back (especially cigarette burns) • has hair pulled out • broken arms (especially spiral fractures) or a broken jaw • is chronically dirty and unkempt, or teeth are covered by plaque • is infected by parasites or fungus, has sores, and is not being appropriately treated • shows evidence of dehydration or malnutrition • serious height and weight abnormalities • needs a hearing aide or consistently comes to school without it, or who needs glasses and no effort is being made to provide them or repair them if broken • has serious cuts, burns, bruises • who fails to thrive for no apparent reason • shows signs of being anorexic or bulimic • exhibits signs psychosomatic illness.

Obviously, many of the signs listed in Figures 4.1 and 4.2 of possible physical abuse or neglect may be the result of conditions other than intentional parental maltreatment. However, instances of any physical trauma should immediately be reported to the school nurse or other appropriate official. Other than in a clear medical emergency, school staff, except for nurses, should never treat injuries or take the child to a physician without proper (which usually means parental) consent.

Although child neglect can be as serious (or more serious) as some physical injuries, neglect often goes undetected or unreported. Educators are oftentimes uncomfortable when they see what may be material neglect but which they think is related to an impoverished home environment. Being aware of the difficulties associated with raising a family under circumstances of poverty or strife, they may believe that calling attention to possible neglect due to lack of resources is both unfair and cruel. Not to do so, however, is potentially far more damaging. One of the prime reasons for reporting these conditions — whatever the cause — is to place parents in touch with resources that will help them.

Keep Records

Very often there are marginal cases which may not arouse the educator's immediate suspicion. Sometimes it takes a period of weeks or months before a teacher or staff member has reasonable cause to suspect maltreatment. It is helpful, therefore, to keep a dated record book with which to document observations made both before and after reporting.

If a staff member should report a borderline case which later proves to be invalid, he or she should not feel guilty. A referral merely suggests the possibility of abuse, neglect, or some other undesirable condition that may require attention. It may also put families in touch with resources which will help them.

WHEN OBSERVING PARENTS

We educators should be cautious in our judgments about whether our students' parents are abusive until verified information is available. Indeed, we should suspend judgment altogether until we are informed by trained experts who have studied the parents as well as the referred child. In addition to visiting the home, involving health experts, and talking to others, child protection investigators will look to school staff (especially teachers and nurses) for their observations of both the parents and the children.

Many experts suggests that the presence of child abuse or neglect should be considered a possibility when parents exhibit signs which are listed in Figure 4.3. We suggest this list as guidelines, but as in the case of observing signs in children, serious caution is in order. We must consider the total picture and when we are suspicious we need to receive confirmation from professional resources.

Once again, caution should be taken; many parents who are not abusive exhibit some of these same signs. Nevertheless, when one notes these signs, the hypothesis of

Figure 4.3
Possible Signs Among Parents

- indicate that they were themselves abused;
- consistently ignore their child, or show detachment;
- react with extreme impatience and anger in addressing their child's normal needs;
- indicate that their child is very "bad" or "different;"
- appear to be suffering from a mental disorder;
- appear cruel or sadistic or lack remorse for any harm they inflict;
- indicate there is no one to help relieve them of their "burdens;"
- show evidence of being out of control, or express fear of losing control;
- present a contradictory history of the child's condition, or present a history that fails to explain their child's injury;
- unduly delay in seeking medical care for their child;
- reveal inappropriate awareness of seriousness of situation (either overreaction or underreaction);
- continue to complain about irrelevant problems unrelated to the injury or to the child's needs;
- are abusing drugs or alcohol;
- are reluctant to give information relevant to their child's injury or needs;
- refuse consent for diagnostic studies despite need;
- hospital "shop" or constantly go to different physicians to treat the child's injuries;
- hold unrealistic expectations for their child's performance or achievement, or who devalue their child's legitimate accomplishments;
- do not demonstrate any affection for their child;
- are willing to use their child in custody or other battles, regardless of the harm this causes the child.

abuse or neglect should be considered and reported for final verification or rejection by others.

> **Child protective services personnel emphasize that they are looking for *patterns*, not isolated behaviors, when they attempt to identify abuse or neglect.**

UNDERSTANDING
PSYCHOLOGICAL ABUSE

To date, the bulk of research on child maltreatment has focused on physical abuse, physical neglect, and sexual abuse of children and adolescents. However, the examination of these forms of maltreatment does not fully address the emotional and cognitive consequences of abuse. Yet for most abused children, "psychological" or "emotional" abuse is perhaps the most critical aspect of their lives.

> **Psychological damage is a core consequence of sexual abuse, physical abuse and neglect, as well as being a form of abuse in its own right.**

It is the psychological aspects of parent-child relationships, expressed in terms of how children learn to think about themselves and interact with others, that is central in understanding whether a pattern of behavior is abusive. For example, long after the physical damage has healed, a battered child can suffer from diminished self-conceptions and impaired social competencies.

Garbarino and associates assert that: "Rather than casting psychological maltreatment as an ancillary issue, subordinate to other forms of abuse and neglect, we should place it as the centerpiece of efforts to understand family functioning and to protect children. In almost all cases, it is the psychological consequences of an act that define that act as abusive." (1986: 7)

"Psychological maltreatment is the core issue in the broader picture of abuse and neglect. It provides the unifying theme and is the critical aspect in the overwhelming majority of what appear as physical and sexual maltreatment cases." (1986: 8)

The lack of attention given to the problem of psychological abuse, however, is understandable. Child abuse experts as a group generally have failed to specify how psychological abuse is to be measured. In other words, they have not provided a consensus as to what psychological abuse is, apart from a variety of conjectural theories. Perhaps that is why psychological abuse is one of the least likely forms of maltreatment to be reported.

While we all agree that certain blatant actions of a parent can be emotionally damaging to the child (e.g., torturing the child's pet as a means of punishing the child), what else can we say to shed light on the problem? First, most experts agree that psychological abuse can be both active and passive; it includes behavior ranging from deliberate humiliation and belittlement, cruel verbal assaults and terrorizing, to a withdrawal from interaction and a withholding of affection.

Second, it is usually agreed that while harsh or degrading nonphysical punishment for misbehavior may temporarily cause youngsters to behave as desired, harm may be done in terms of the child's self-conceptions and social and intellectual competencies. It is easy to overlook such harm because the negative psychological impact of abuse on children tends to be gradual in its development. Psychological damage is often subtle and not recognized by others until self-esteem and intellectual and social competencies are seriously eroded.

According to Garbarino and associates (1986: 8), emotionally destructive actions of caretakers can take the following five forms. Educators and others should pay special attention to parents who respond to their children by:

1. **Rejecting** (the adult refuses to acknowledge the child's worth and the legitimacy of the child's needs).

2. **Isolating** (the adult cuts the child off from normal social experiences, prevents the child from forming friendships, and makes the child believe that he or she is alone in the world).

3. **Terrorizing** (the adult verbally assaults the child, creates a climate of fear, bullies and frightens the child, and makes the child believe that the world is capricious and hostile).

4. **Ignoring** (the adult deprives the child of essential stimulation and responsiveness, stifling emotional growth and intellectual development).

5. **Corrupting** (the adult "mis-socializes" the child, stimulates the child to engage in destructive antisocial behavior, reinforces that deviance, and makes the child unfit for normal social experience).

Taken together, these kinds of actions by caretakers undermine or destroy the foundations of self which make one a socially and intellectually competent human being. Specifically, one's feelings of safety, trust, autonomy and control—that which is necessary for competent functioning as a social being—are threatened. All too often the final result of psychological abuse is to produce emotionally impaired individuals unable to function with even the minimal competencies necessary for healthy lives. Another equally tragic result may be to produce future victimizers who, as adults, reproduce these behaviors in interactions with their mates and their children.

Educators should be especially alert to signs of child abuse in those families known to be highly unstable and undergoing stress, particularly if there is a known history of abuse. Regardless of the cues which trigger one's suspicions of physical, sexual or psychological abuse, the responsibility of the observer is to set in motion a process of confirmation and intervention on behalf of young survivors of abuse. Knowing how to identify abuse is the first step in that process.

5
INCEST

In North America, estimates of sexually abusive behavior between adults and children vary dramatically, and range between 200,000 and possibly as many as 10 million cases per year. Perhaps as many as one-in-five females, and one-in-ten males have had at least one sexually abusive experience as children, usually by a member of the family. It is also estimated that nearly 38 million adults in the United States and Canada were sexually abused as children.

While it is impossible to determine the exact incidence of incest, we do know that the number of victims is huge. We also know that the number of reported cases has risen steadily over the past decade. Furthermore, evidence consistently shows that sexual abuse cases involve parents and surrogate parents more than strangers. In only about three to ten percent of sexual abuse cases are the perpetrators strangers to their victims.

PATTERNS OF INCEST

Incest differs from physical abuse in several important respects.

- Incest tends to be premeditated while physical abuse tends to be more spontaneous.

- Incest is a serious taboo. Sexual abuse of children and teenagers engenders such intense feelings of moral outrage that impartiality is difficult. Although there is variation in what people think about different sexual practices, our society has established stringent taboos against incest and other forms of sexual contact between adults and children.

- Incest ranges in type from simple assault, i.e., non-coital sexual contact, involving sexually explicit erotic vocabulary, to forcible battery of a child.

This is illustrated in Figure 5.1. The extent of emotional damage to victims is likely to be much greater than results from physical abuse alone, but as shown in Figure 5.1, it too ranges in accord with the type of incest experienced.

Whereas a large portion of society supports the practice of hitting children in the name of discipline, most people do not condone incest. Both the hitting of children and incest, however, are alike in that they tend to occur over an extended period of time (months or years).

Sources of Incest

Stepfathers, surrogate fathers, and biological fathers are by far the most common sexual abusers of children,

Figure 5.1
Types of Incestuous Assault Against
Children and Adolescents*

Sexual Molestation

- Non-coital sexual contact

- Results in sexual stimulation of offender

- Includes petting, fondling

- Includes exhibitionism (exposure of offender's sexual organs)

- Includes voyeurism (watching victim undress, nude)

LEAST DAMAGING

Involves different treatment plans, prognoses, ages, time sequences, consequences (legal and psychological), and dynamics (homosexual, heterosexual, close relative, distant relative, related by marriage).

Sexual Assault

- Manual-oral and/or genital contact with genitals of victim

- Non-consent

- Includes masturbatory activities, fellatio, cunnilingus

Forcible Rape

- Forced sexual contact resulting in assault with penis

- Uses fear, violence, fraud, threats

MOST DAMAGING

From Mayer, Adele. *Incest* (2nd ed.) Holmes Beach, FL: Learning Publications, Inc., 1993.

accounting for over ninety percent of the reported cases. Mother-son or mother-daughter sexual relationships are relatively rare. Even when mothers are involved in incest, it is often at the urging of an adult male who participates in the sexual abuse (Mayer, 1991).

Given the high proportion of stepfather and surrogate father involvement, the increasing number of children living under this arrangement is noteworthy. Over half of all eighteen-year-olds have lived parts of their lives in a family with a stepfather or surrogate father. With the current increase in single parent families, the risks to children and adolescents may be increasing, and this may in part explain the steady increase in reported cases of sexual abuse.

The onset of incest can begin at any age and can happen to males as well as to females. However, the "typical" victim of incest is a female between the ages of eight and twelve. From the first experience, she is made to continue in a pattern of victimization which lasts over a prolonged period of time.

Younger incest victims are likely to experience fondling, oral-genital stimulation, and exhibitionism more often than penetration. Then teenagers, unlike younger children, are likely to experience penetration.

> **Typically, physical violence is not used to force children to participate in sexual acts. Rather, threats of rejection or loss of love, deception, and making the victim feel guilty and responsible, are the most common means of forcing participation.**

There are at least two reasons for a general absence of physical force in incest. In the first case, incestuous fathers need to enlist the cooperation of their children to keep them available as sexual "partners" for an extended period of time, and not leave any physical evidence which might lead to discovery. For this reason, penetration is less common with younger children because it does increase the risk of detectable physical damage. To physically damage one's child in an observable way would diminish the chances of such cooperation and increase the likelihood of discovery.

Second, children and teenagers are susceptible to a parent's position of psychological, physical and material dominance. Incestuous parents use loyalty, trust, fear and dependence as weapons to force their children into sexual activity and to ensure their silence. With such an arsenal of psychological weapons to manipulate the victim, physical force generally is not required. Nevertheless, such insidious psychological violence can be even more devastating than an act of physical aggression.

The fear of possible family disintegration also may serve as motivation for a victim's cooperation with an incestuous parent. Such fear is a frequently cited reason why victims of incest fail to divulge their having been sexually abused. They are seeking to protect the family from stigma and legal complications, and they fear that they would be responsible for "destroying" the family. Hence, they endure the abuse, often for prolonged periods. This is not to suggest in any way that child or teenage victims of incest give their consent, or are responsible for sexual involvement with their parents.

> **There is no solid research evidence to suggest that children instigate incestuous liaisons with their parents.**

Myths about Incest

As in the case of rape, there are stereotypes and false assumptions concerning the degree of victim-precipitation of the incest experience. Some have incorrectly asserted that incest victims are being "seductive" or are spontaneously acting out sexual fantasies. Similarly offered is the false observation that children enjoy the "special attention" of incest and therefore bear partial responsibility. Some false claims are made purporting that daughters welcome the sexual advances of their fathers as an indication of parental love.

Given the age, maturity, and resources of children, meaningful consent to engage in sexual practices with their parents is not legally or morally possible. Children are not responsible for incest; adult offenders are. It is the adults who misuse their power, and it is their children who pay the price of that abuse.

> **Adult abusers use their position of power to instigate incest, to continue the practice once it has started, to keep their behavior secret, and ultimately to blame their victims for what happened.**

Another popular (though untested) belief places responsibility on the mother for father-daughter incest.

This theory purports that it is the mother's "unconscious desire" to place the daughter in the role of wife and lover, thus relieving herself of this responsibility. According to this false argument, by abandoning her responsibilities as a wife and mother, the mother pushes the father and daughter into a sexual relationship.

In truth, research supports the view that the overwhelming majority of mothers do not consciously or unconsciously encourage their partners to enter into incestuous relationships with their daughters (Ovaris, 1991). Indeed, the majority of mothers are unaware that incest is taking place and are deeply shocked when they learn what has happened.

The untested theory that mothers initiate or condone the incestuous involvement between fathers and daughters carries a sexist overtone. The sexist overtone is that of blaming women for the inappropriate conduct of men. Such a sexist attitude makes it difficult to help victims and their families. This argument also fails to explain male victims of incest.

Restated, while it is true that incest is indicative of a breakdown of the family, neither children nor non-offending mothers cause this breakdown. It is true that in some cases mothers or other family members eventually come to know about incestuous relationships and, for a variety of reasons, they reject or fail to act upon such knowledge. However, even when they fail to act against the offending adult, to blame the woman or child and not the perpetrator for the incest is inappropriate.

CONTRIBUTING CONDITIONS

Although simple theories concerning the causes of incest abound, the problem is complex. No single explanation is sufficient to account for all cases. There are differences between and among perpetrators, victims, and family interaction patterns. Nonetheless, there are certain conditions that are relatively common to incest situations. These include psychological isolation, stress, and alcohol abuse.

Psychological Isolation

Similar to the pattern of physical abuse cases, isolation is frequently cited as contributing to incest. Isolation does not necessarily mean physical separation, but rather is determined by the lack of close friendships outside the family. In many cases, an overly heavy dependence upon one another within the family to meet all emotional needs appears to be crucial. Often there is deep suspicion of "outsiders." Also, once a pattern of incest begins, feared stigma of public disclosure tends to further isolate the family.

> **Social isolation intensifies the incestuous pattern and reduces the likelihood of outside intervention.**

Some argue that a lack of "legitimate" sexual outlets can result in the development of incest within the family. Most offending fathers, however, have "legitimate" sexual outlets, but nonetheless choose to sexually misuse their children. Sexual dysfunction in a marriage is not the cause of incest; selfishness is. However, the presence of incest can produce sexual difficulties in a marriage, and can greatly complicate the development of healthy sexual patterns among victims as they mature.

With incest perpetrators who are genetically related to their victims, usually it is not a generalized pedophilic craving for children that initially leads to incest, though such a craving may subsequently develop. In the case of stepparents, however, pedophilia is a somewhat more common motivating factor. A pedophile sometimes marries or lives with a woman for the purpose of gaining access to her children. It is also true that many perpetrators were themselves victims of sexual abuse as children, though this is certainly no excuse for continuing to inflict such behaviors on others.

Given the lack of an external support system, there is heavy dependence on family members to meet emotional and sexual needs. However, isolation is not a true "cause" of incest. Rather, isolation constitutes a background condition which makes the emergence of incest possible. Isolation provides an opportunity for parents who use their children for sexual gratification to act in secrecy.

Alcohol

Another common element in incest is alcohol abuse. As many as fifty percent of reported cases of incest involve an alcohol abusing father. As in the case of physical abuse, however, it is false to assume that alcohol "causes" the incestuous behavior. Rather, alcohol lowers inhibitions and provides a convenient excuse or face-saving rationalization for the conduct. Abusers employ this as an excuse to deny their conduct and to absolve themselves from responsibility for their actions. It is as if they say to themselves, "I'm not really like that . . . the alcohol made me do it."

> **Like other personal maladjustment problems, alcohol abuse may be as much a result as it is a "cause" of incest. Being drunk is not a legal or moral justification for sexual abuse. Furthermore, most fathers who drink do not molest their children.**

Climates of Stress

The occurrence of incest is both symptomatic of, and a catalyst for, family stress. Marital discord and sexual incompatibility between husband and wife, economic difficulty, illness, prolonged absence followed by the return of the father, fear of abandonment, family disintegration, and the death of a spouse, have all been cited as reasons for incest. Stress alone, however, does not cause incest. There are too many people who experience extreme stress, without incest, to accept such an explanation.

> **Rather than stress causing incest, it is more accurate to say that the presence of incest is a *source* of extreme stress within a family.**

We know that most incestuous parents experience considerable personal problems. The observation of such tensions and personal problems may be the basis of a popular view that mental illness is the reason for incest. Contrary to popular belief, however, there is little evidence to suggest that mental illness is the cause. Perpetrators are neither psychotic nor delusional, but rather very calculating and intentional in their actions. Nevertheless, the fear, shame, guilt and low self-esteem associated with incest add considerable psychological stress to victims, to offenders, and to other family members.

In other words, psychological problems are as likely to be a result of incest as a cause. No doubt the guilt and shame of offenders help to explain their relatively high suicide rate if their actions are discovered.

EFFECTS OF SEXUAL ABUSE

Controversy exists over whether or not young children and teenagers are seriously harmed by having their parents exploit them sexually. A few argue that the "innocence of youth" protects them against harm; that since young people are vague about what society expects, they are not traumatized by violations. For example, as Kinsey (1953) is often cited, "it is difficult to understand why a child, except for its cultural conditioning, should be disturbed at having its genitals touched, or disturbed at seeing the genitals of other persons." There is overwhelming evidence, however, that children and adolescents are profoundly harmed when they are sexually exploited.

Most people have been taught that incest is wrong. That is why adolescents and adults who experienced incest are so secretive. Of course, most therapists recognize that participating in an event which is a major societal taboo can cause deep psychological problems.

In fact, most mental health workers and researchers report that incest victims suffer so much that they are impaired long into adulthood. Furthermore, the psychological consequences of incest are likely to be worse than those due to rape by strangers. The extensive confusion, fear, shame, low self-esteem and thoughts of suicide among incest victims are evidence of severe damage. Studies indicate that a high percentage of women who undergo psychiatric treatment were sexually exploited during their childhood or adolescence. Running away, substance abuse, delinquency, self-mutilation, and long-term sexual dysfunction are also possible outcomes of being sexually abused.

Unlike the effects of physical abuse and neglect, there are comparatively few obvious signs associated with a sexually maltreated child or teenager. Furthermore, incest victims are usually protective of their families and are not likely to be forthcoming about their experiences. When incestuous experiences are revealed, the revelations usually occur during a time when there is confrontation and crisis in the family. For instance, an adolescent may divulge incest if she has a fight with her father over her desires to date, or if her father initiates her younger sisters into incest.

Adolescent males who are sexually abused are especially prone to be secretive. Males in our society are expected to be able to protect themselves. To "allow" oneself to be violated is seen by the young male as a personal failure and as an indication of "weakness." Certainly, one does not make such a perceived failure public.

Further compounding the problem of male victims is the fact that nearly always the perpetrator is an older male. This adds great confusion to the male youngster's sense of sexual identity. Thus, adolescent males who are sexually exploited feel a double loss: they have lost their "manly" ability to defend themselves and they have lost their "manhood" in terms of their emerging sexuality. The stigma is such that many would rather endure a private hell than to suffer the public humiliation of what they perceive as their failure.

If young males or females reveal sexual assault, there may be a tendency among adults to disregard their accounts. Unfortunately, Freud argued that children are prone to incestuous fantasies. As a result of this assertion about childhood fantasies, a child's truthful revelation of sexual involvement with a parent may be interpreted as a fabrication or as an expression of fantasy.

More recently, there are claims that children are being "implanted" with "false memories" of sexual abuse. The research on the role of suggestion (by therapists and others) in creating false recollections of abuse is highly equivocal. Even if the phenomenon does exist — and that is a source of debate — research on these false memories has been conducted on non-traumatized populations. Most evidence on children and adolescents who are traumatized by abuse fails to substantiate the case for false memories. The issue, however, is yet to be resolved.

Some have argued that sexual abuse prevention programs in schools contribute to false reports. There is almost no evidence to support this assertion. In fact, the data show that a very small percentage of child or teenage initiated reports of sexual abuse are false, and that school programs are helpful in bringing abuse cases to the attention of authorities.

The problem is compounded if victims retract their account upon further questioning. Such retractions occur because young people are terrified by the possible breakup of their families, by the embarrassment they will face with their friends, by a sense of shame, and by the feared severity of the punishment that they or their parents will receive.

In addition, in the interim between a report of incest and its investigation, the abusive parent has ample time to construct a "cover story" and to pressure the child or teenager into denial. In such cases, the young person now bears a double burden of stigma. First, the child feels the guilt and responsibility for having gone public, thus possibly jeopardizing the family. Second, the child must now contend with adults and others outside the family who may believe that he or she has a penchant for "telling stories." Yet experts agree that only a small fraction of child initiated reports of sexual abuse are false.

> **There is little reason for children to make up stories about being victims, and a great many reasons for offenders to deny their actions.**

Regardless of whether or not a victim reveals incest or other sexual assault, several cues exist for astute observers to use in discovering sexual maltreatment. To some extent, the physical and behavioral symptoms vary with the age of the victim. While no single characteristic is sufficient evidence of incest, a pattern of symptoms should raise the specter of its existence. The following are physical and behavioral characteristics commonly seen among sexual abuse victims:

- behavioral problems such as running away, truancy, substance abuse, a drop in school performance, being withdrawn or highly aggressive, and fits of crying;

- inability to establish positive relationships with peers;

- talk of being "dirty" or "damaged," excessive bathing, and very low self-esteem;

- blurting out sexually oriented remarks that seem inappropriate or unlikely considering the person's age or the circumstances;

- drawings or gestures in the context of play that are suggestive of sexual experiences;

- unexplained pregnancy (e.g., where there is no boyfriend);

- being "starved for affection" or seeking inappropriate and provocative physical contact (e.g., a child or young adolescent "French kissing" an adult);

- sexual promiscuity and prostitution;

- frequent bacterial infection, genital rash, pain in the genital area, enuresis, rectal bleeding, venereal disease or chronic vaginal discharge;

- phobias, fear of adults, hysterical seizures, nightmares, psychosomatic illness;

- severe depression, self-mutilation, and suicide attempts.

Teachers, school nurses, counselors and others should pay special attention to students who are in high risk groups. Those who are physically or mentally handicapped represent one such high risk category. (Their peers may take sexual advantage of them, as do some parents.) Also, in families where there is a previous history of child sexual abuse by a parent, the younger children may become targets. Similarly, where there is frequent shifting of stepparents or live-in surrogates, the risk of sexual abuse seems to be greater. Where the mother is absent and the surrogate father or biological father is in close, secluded proximity with the daughter for long periods of time, the risk of sexual abuse can increase, especially if the adult is known to have a history of sexual abuse in his childhood.

In the case of an adolescent female, an incestuous relationship may come to light if she becomes pregnant. Although statistics vary, as many as seven-to-ten percent of female adolescent incest victims become pregnant. Not only does this increase the risk of genetic problems if the pregnancy is carried to term, but the psychological risks to the victim are heightened by such a pregnancy, regardless of whether or not the baby is born.

Variables such as age, frequency of occurrence, and degree of physical force, are key factors in the amount of harm done to victims. Many juveniles who run away from home, many youths involved in delinquency, large numbers of adolescent prostitutes, and many others who have emotional problems and have experienced sexual abuse, need the special attention and care of therapists if their problems are to be reduced.

Therefore it is of paramount importance that everyone understand the damage that can be done by parents who use their children to satisfy their sexual desires. It is also critical to get special professional help for victims of sexual abuse. Finally, instructing students about sexually appropriate behaviors, and instilling in them the values and skills needed to be effective parents, represent important contributions educators can make toward sexual abuse prevention.

Part B
Secondary
Prevention

6
INTERVENTION
POLICIES

If intervention efforts to help abused children are to succeed, then procedures and responsibilities must be spelled out and communicated to teachers, school counselors, administrators and others throughout the school system. Failure to establish clearly understood policies may inadvertently commit the staff to inaction.

While the need to develop intervention policies in school is imperative, failure to implement them may be worse than no policy at all. This is especially true if such policies communicate the idea that action is being taken, yet there is no real change in outcome. Responses to child abuse should be more than symbolic. Most educators know that many excellent policies can be sabotaged, misunderstood, or simply ignored. It is often easy to create the illusion of action by formulating a policy on paper. Yet an equally important task is to elicit the system-wide cooperation needed to ensure policy implementation.

An early step in planning an intervention program is to discuss two broad areas of concern: 1) how to achieve a workable intervention policy; and 2) clarifying the goals that the policy might include. The final outcome may emerge as something not anticipated. But uniting people who have a genuine interest in the problem — not just those who are directed to be involved — is crucial to effective policy implementation.

POLICY FORMATION

Because unilateral action in establishing policies is usually unsuccessful, it is important to develop a working network composed of school staff and service agency personnel. The causes and consequences of child abuse and neglect are so complex that neither school, health delivery, law enforcement, government, social services, nor other organizations, alone can effectively respond unless they collaborate. They must share resources, and foster implementation. We think such collaboration is best facilitated with a community coordinating agency that is specifically charged with that responsibility. Unless there is planning and collaboration "turf wars," petty jealousies, and conflict are likely. However, once a collective community force is in action, then it is up to each institution to develop its own task force to provide for how it will intervene when child abuse is suspected or documented. But here again, the school task forces should see themselves as parts of a team with a community coordination agency as the prime source for direction when addressing intervention.

Developing School Task Forces

Effective child protection depends upon breaking down the isolation between diverse elements within the school system and the community. To promote cooperation, the central administration of each school district should assume responsibility for establishing a number of task force committees or teams composed of representatives from all the different groups involved in child protection (e.g., law, health, social work, education). The highest school operations officer (e.g., the superintendent of schools), because of his or her leadership skills and ability to direct resources, should organize the formation of interdisciplinary task force committees. Of course, this should be done with the approval of the school board. In addition, this should be done with the assistance of those who already have a legal mandate to ensure the welfare of children.

Optimum size for a working group seems to be five-to-eight members. Care should be taken to avoid forming committees dominated by one professional area (e.g., medicine, counseling, elementary teaching, social work). Community volunteer groups also should be included if there is an indication of interest. The main criteria for task force membership should be competence, commitment, and the ability to help accomplish team goals.

In cases where a network of child abuse committees is already operating, care should be taken to make certain that they continue to function properly. Often committees that once were active become inactive over time. They exist on paper but no longer function.

> **It is the responsibility of school leaders to make certain that the child abuse committee structure remains active.**

The purpose of these task force committees is to make policy recommendations about reporting, follow-up, support services, inservice training, parent education, and cooperation with human service agencies. The best way to accomplish this is to make sure that the different agencies, professional groups and others at each level of the child protective network have input during the policy-making phase. Oftentimes those who are expected to carry out a policy will feel no vested interest or enthusiasm for doing so unless they have input in the creation of that policy.

Groups at various levels, not just administrators, should help to determine legitimate problems and plans for collective action. Thus it is important for each school district to solicit ideas and feedback from all those who will be involved in the day-to-day implementation of the child protective policy. This promotes a feeling of personal accountability and pride in the overall success of the program. The greater the input from various sectors in the network, the less potential for apathy or opposition to the program.

In addition to making policy recommendations, the purpose of task force committees is to identify problem areas, to offer suggestions about programming needs, and to build a coalition of leaders who support program initiatives. In attempting to develop a comprehensive program, however, task force members should be aware of several obstacles to effective collaboration. The following problems are likely to be present in most communities. Knowledge of these difficulties can help reduce potential conflicts which could undermine program implementation.

Anticipating Roadblocks

Most roadblocks to effective collaboration share a common theme: poor communication. If the character of communication between task force members is negative, then there is little hope of effective collaboration. The only things likely to be generated are paperwork, cynicism and finger pointing. This is deadly to creating effective intervention programs.

Task force members (particularly the leaders) should anticipate several potential obstacles to positive communication. They need to:

- Be aware that members may have conflicting agendas. Issues of turf protection, of division of responsibilities, and of program "ownership" can emerge at any time.

- Be sensitive to any past conflicts between team members (especially between school and protective services personnel). Such conflicts are not likely to be forgotten and can undermine trust. Some may claim that "we are already doing these things," while others question the success of such efforts. As a result, when innovative suggestions are made, some may interpret these suggestions as a vote of "no confidence" regarding what they claim to be doing already.

- Anticipate that some will claim expertise in areas where they have little training or experience. For example, knowing friends or students who are abuse victims does not make an educator an instant expert on the problems of child maltreatment.

- Understand the need for all those involved in the project to secure a valuable but intangible asset — public recognition for their work. Pride in what one is doing (or has accomplished) should not be seen as unwanted, but rather as an asset which can be channeled into strong commitment.

Because child abuse intervention programs necessarily involve both school staff and community human services personnel, task force members should anticipate complaints emerging from each group. Complaints which school staff commonly register about protective services may include the following:

- Delays in responding to referrals from schools.

- Inappropriate or incompetent investigation of families.

- Lack of follow-up from agencies regarding the status of a case after a referral has been made.

- No communication from agencies regarding students in special treatment when the school did not make the referral (e.g., a new student who is in treatment for sexual abuse).

- Not knowing which services are offered by which agencies, and not being able to evaluate or to distinguish between services where there is duplication.

- Lack of a continuing, predictable relationship with agency representatives involved in case management.

- A perception that the networking relationship between schools and agencies — and between the agencies themselves — is weak and in need of improvement.

- A belief that human service agencies fail to meet the long-term needs of many individuals and families referred to them (e.g., indigent clients).

For their part, agency personnel serving families in crisis often take umbrage at these criticisms. They cite concerns over confidentiality, large case loads, and limited resources as reasons for these problems. Furthermore, agency representatives often argue that educators contribute to problems in the following ways:

- Those in need are not consistently identified at school or referred to the appropriate agency.

- School personnel lack training in how to identify youth in crisis and how to make an appropriate referral.

- School administrators have not made inservice training in child abuse intervention a priority.

- Schools do not always take advantage of agencies willing to assist in teacher training, even when contacted by agency staff who offer their services.

Solutions

Each community will vary in the extent to which the above issues come into play. There are several strategies, however, that task force leaders and members can employ to avoid problems in cooperation.

- Acknowledge from the beginning that there may be differing agendas and experiences that people bring with them, but this is a strength rather than a limitation. The best way to achieve the common goal of child abuse intervention is to draw upon the diverse talents and resources available, regardless of where they are found.

- Do not refer to past failures or animosity between groups. Emphasize instead examples of successful collaboration in your own community and elsewhere.

- Establish as an objective regularly scheduled dialogues between school and agency representatives. Include topics ranging from the success of information sharing to collaboration on inservice training.

- Designate at least one person to serve as a liaison between schools and agencies. This increases the probabilities that timely information exchange and follow-up will take place when referrals are made.

- Distribute to educators a resource booklet listing agencies, services, and contact persons for making referrals.

- Establish as a goal, district wide school inservices on crisis identification and referral. Agency inservices also should emphasize the special problems confronting teachers, school counselors and others who work with at-risk youth and their parents.

- Establish as a priority a "networking" approach to students known to be at high risk. This should include the coordination of programming in the school when services are provided by agencies. If possible, this should also include the involvement of agency based case managers serving as client advocates.

- Delineate the spheres of competence regarding intervention efforts. For example, educators are likely to be resentful if community agency personnel tell teachers how and what to be teaching students, how to run school based peer assistance programs, or how to instruct a particular student. Similarly, agency staff are likely to be resentful if school personnel who are not trained in mental health offer advice on clinical techniques or appropriate therapies for students in treatment. While it is important to share information in a case management sense, it is also important to guard against stepping beyond one's sphere of competence.

- Do not add new school intervention programs at the expense of other valuable programs or services. Child abuse intervention is not a zero sum game where there are winners and losers. If new school programs or services can be incorporated into an existing structure, the tendency for staff to resist change is reduced.

Providing Necessary Resources

In order to assist task force members in carrying out their duties, the central administration, in conjunction with child protection agencies in each district, should provide a number of supportive services. For example, copies of state or province statutes on child abuse and neglect should be compiled in advance and distributed to each person serving on a committee. Fact sheets on the incidence of child abuse and neglect in the community, as well as lists of resource persons willing to serve as consultants or volunteers, could be assembled. Providing the committees with secretarial assistance and a place where materials can be typed and printed also would help.

The importance of cooperative involvements with community, state and federal public and private agencies will be recognized in the development of resources. Child protective agencies will have available brochures, literature and films, and often will arrange for experts to visit schools and speak on topics of child abuse and neglect. Schools should not fail to make use of the many people and agencies already available in the community who can be of assistance.

Create a Coordinating Council

In addition to forming a series of interdisciplinary committees designed to make policy recommendations about child protection, the central administration should create a coordinating council composed of representatives from the school system and all the appropriate child service groups in the community. This coordinating council should receive recommendations from the various committees and assume responsibility for writing and periodically reviewing school policies. This council, in collaboration with the school district administration, should be responsible for integrating the manifold activities of the diverse task forces.

Although the coordinating council represents a centralized policy-making body, its functioning is based upon the decentralized operations of constituents throughout all levels of the system. Ideally, this arrangement will enhance inter-agency communication. It should also promote efficient service use and greater participation in carrying out the policy. The ultimate goal is to write a child protection policy that can be readily implemented in schools.

Avoid Issuing Edicts

The child abuse policy should not be perceived as an edict imposed on school staff from above. Simply the appearance of an autocratic approach can alienate those whose support is crucial.

The policy should be seen as emerging from the collaborative efforts of school building staff, central administrative and agency personnel, with the central administration merely coordinating these efforts. An approach which involves lower echelon people who are necessary to implement policy has the greatest chance of promoting accountability. If people feel that they meaningfully participate in creating a policy, then they are more likely to take pride and interest in guaranteeing the successful implementation of that policy.

Staff at all levels of the school system should be encouraged to provide feedback regarding successes or difficulties in making the policy work. The policy should allow for possible revision in light of this feedback.

Administrators should discuss with subordinates potential changes in task directives and provide support to encourage their involvement. All too often persons in leadership positions vociferously condemn errors in policy execution, thereby stifling necessary feedback from the lower echelons. Generous praise can go a long way toward building the kind of feedback network necessary to achieve an effective policy.

POLICY COMPONENTS

A policy should not be considered too fixed or rigid by those who must put it into operation. The policy on child abuse and neglect should be flexible enough for adoption throughout the system. It should also be subject to periodic review and revision. Successful policies usually have the following in common.

A Policy Rationale

The policy statement should begin by providing a brief rationale explaining the need for school personnel to recognize and report child abuse. Included in this rationale should be up-to-date community statistics on child abuse and neglect. An ad hoc committee of the task force should be set up to do a thorough study of available community data. This information will be of great value in later evaluations. The policy statement should also emphasize the pedagogical and humanitarian reasons for involving educators in child abuse intervention.

Clarify Legal Obligations

The policy statement should clarify the statutes and regulations regarding abuse and neglect as they impact on the school district. This section should include a discussion of: 1) the legal definitions of child abuse and neglect; 2) the legal obligations to report suspected cases of abuse and neglect; 3) the legal immunities from civil or criminal liability for those who report or participate in investigative proceedings; and 4) the limits of the law in terms of what interventions school staff may or may not engage in when confronting abused children and their parents.

Educators should know that all laws provide for confidentiality and protection for "good faith" reporting, and that failure to report can result in court action. Thus, the statement should indicate possible actions to be taken for failing to report, as well as policies regarding confidentiality of report records. Those agencies responsible for dealing with abuse and neglect (e.g., child protective agencies, court and police) should be consulted in developing this component of the policy.

Specify When to Report

The policy statement should specify the conditions which justify a report. Several chapters of this book list symptoms which alert teachers and others to the possibility of physical abuse, sexual abuse, physical neglect and psychological abuse. Inservice training on identification and reporting should be a part of every school's program.

It is also imperative that the policy statement specify the following:

- the method by which school personnel are to report;

- the person or persons mandated to file reports;

- the person or agency receiving reports;

- the person responsible for follow-up;

- the professional ethics of reporting (e.g., confidentiality).

Building Teams and Coordinators

Included in the next chapter is an illustration of the use of school building child abuse and neglect or CAN Teams. The building CAN Team (about four staff persons) may include a teacher, nurse, counselor, school social worker, school psychologist or other staff persons who regularly work in the building. The team's coordinator may be the principal or someone appointed by the principal.

Guidelines should be formulated for the CAN Teams in the following areas:

- procedure for gathering data if abuse or neglect is suspected;

- procedures for receiving and reporting information to outside agencies;

- coordinating school staff activities in confirmed cases of child abuse or neglect;

- providing feedback to school staff regarding referrals;

- developing workshops and inservice training to facilitate intervention programming.

We believe that building CAN Teams are so important that a statement strongly requesting their support should be included in the written policy. In the absence of CAN Teams, the principal in each building should address the above tasks.

Specifying Procedures for Reporting

Classroom teachers, teacher-aides and physical education staff are often in an advantageous position to initially observe suspected cases of abuse and neglect. It is our recommendation, however, that school policies absolve them from the responsibility of filing the report. The demands on a teacher's time and energies are great enough without having to fear possible reprisals from parents. There have been instances of parents threatening or attacking teachers who have reported children as possibly abused. Equally important, there may come a time when the teacher must work with the parents on educational matters. This requires cooperation without undo feelings of tension.

The policy statement should specify that the principal, school nurse, or some other school official is responsible for filing the report. However, the policy should clearly state that it is the teacher's duty (as it is every other school staff person's duty) to bring his or her observations to the attention of the school official charged with making the formal report. Following an oral statement, a written report should be filed.

Identifying Community Agencies

The agency designated to receive child abuse and neglect cases should be included in the policy statement (e.g., Child Protective Services). The functions of the protective service agencies and all other agencies such as the courts and police should be specified. Educators should be aware of what agencies are obligated to do, as well as what they cannot do. It is important that those filing reports understand the lines of authority — who has jurisdiction and when — and who should report to whom.

In an ideal situation, schools and agencies complement each other following an abuse report. Problem families are quickly identified, evaluated, and provided with the necessary services. Unfortunately, this will not happen unless school, agency and professional roles are clearly defined. There could be duplication of investigations, confusion and struggle over case jurisdiction, cynicism, poor communication between participants, anxiety among family members, and further danger to children because of delayed services. Many of these potential problems can be avoided if professional role boundaries are specified in the policy statement and if the channels of communication are clear and remain open.

An intervention policy should take into account that child abuse is a multidimensional problem requiring a multidisciplinary approach. Child abuse is not just a school problem, but a problem extending beyond the domain of any single group.

The child protection network we advocate can be built upon existing resources in the school district. By seeking linkages between existing organizations, a team approach will build upon community strengths and establish alliances among those who can provide essential services. Given such linkages, child protection can become a community-wide social movement with troubled families being the ultimate benefactors.

7
REPORTING AND REFERRAL

Effective reporting depends upon the leadership in each building of child abuse and neglect teams (CAN Teams). Likewise, the success of treatment and follow-up care is influenced by the quality of school-community relationships established during the referral phase. In this chapter we examine the referral process and suggest ways of ensuring an effective response to suspected cases of child maltreatment.

THE ADMINISTRATION OF REPORTING

The principal is a critical link in the chain of professionals who respond to the needs of maltreated children. As the school's educational leader, he or she can be expected to assume overall responsibility for managing the school's child abuse and neglect policy. If for some reason this is not possible, the principal should assign this task to a competent professional respected by building staff. The person with the prime responsibility for leadership should have:

- knowledge of reporting procedures at all levels;

- knowledge of the school district's written policy statement for reporting and its implications for school staff;

- skills in managing the school's policy and procedures for reporting cases of abuse and neglect;

- the ability to create a climate of support and trust which enables teachers and other staff to act in a constructive manner; and

- the ability to communicate effectively with parents, teachers, children and protective services regarding the implementation of school policy.

Effective leadership also means eliciting the cooperation of those needed to execute policies. In this regard, a well-informed staff is essential for effective reporting.

Informing Staff of Laws and Regulations

The principal (or the person designated to oversee the reporting process) should meet periodically with staff to acquaint them with child abuse and neglect statutes and policies. It is especially critical that new staff members (e.g., new teachers and teacher aides) be acquainted with reporting procedures. The following questions should be addressed:

- What constitutes child abuse and neglect?

- Who is required to report under the law?

- What types of maltreatment must be reported?

- When should a teacher or staff member report the suspicion of abuse?

- Under what conditions must mandated reporters report?

- What are the legal and professional consequences for reporting or for failing to report?

- What, if anything, are educators required to do beyond reporting?

- What protection for school staff is built into the law and the reporting process?

- Which agency is responsible for investigating and handling child abuse and neglect cases?

- What are the procedures for follow-up?

- What responsibilities do protective service personnel have regarding working with the school following a report?

- What should be done when contacted (or threatened) by a parent who is under investigation for alleged abuse?

School District Reporting Policy

The next step is to inform the staff about the school district's policy and procedures for dealing with abuse cases. Specifically, they need such information as:

- the steps, if any, to be taken prior to reporting;

- the person or persons to whom reports are filed;

- the school's plan of action if abuse is reported;

- the school's role once child protective services has entered the case, including the responsibilities of school personnel during and after the disposition of the case;

- the special procedures which might apply when working with abused children or their parents following a report;

- the procedures for working with protective service agencies assisting parents and children.

Community Agencies

Educators and protective services staff cannot afford to have poor communication or lack of cooperation. This can be prevented, or at least lessened, by inviting child protective case workers to the school to meet and work with the school staff. Joint inservice training is often a beneficial way of establishing a sound working relationship. Face-to-face contact and the exchange of ideas usually promote cooperation and mutual respect.

School personnel can benefit by learning the following from an experienced case worker:

- agency goals and expectations for identifying and reporting cases;

- criteria used by protective services to determine if abuse or neglect is occurring;

- needs of protective services for further information once a case is confirmed;

- relationship between community agencies in regard to reporting, investigation and referral;

- problems faced by the protective services when dealing with various types of cases;

- suggestions to school personnel when confronted with problems in reporting; and

- ways of enhancing school and agency cooperation in case management.

CONFIDENTIALITY OF SCHOOL RECORDS

When meeting with staff, their legal and ethical concerns over confidentiality should be addressed. Legislation exists to protect parents and children from unnecessary and potentially damaging public exposure. This legislation establishes guidelines governing the release of information from school records. In general, if a school record is to be shared outside the school, the consent of parents usually is required.

There are several clear exceptions, however, which make it possible for schools to bypass the requirement of seeking parental consent prior to disclosing information from school records. The general category of "health or safety emergency" constitutes such an exception. To determine if a health and safety emergency condition exists, the following should be considered. They are:

- seriousness of the threat to the immediate health or safety of the student;

- the need for information to meet the emergency;

- possible consequences for failing to treat the situation as an emergency;

- whether the parties to whom the information is to be disclosed are in a position to deal appropriately with the emergency; and

- extent to which time is of the essence in dealing with the emergency.

Child maltreatment is considered to be a health and safety emergency.

Similar to the reporting of infectious disease, mandatory reporting laws require disclosure of abuse and neglect to agencies on a "need to know" basis. The laws are intended to protect children without abrogating parental rights to privacy. The law clearly differentiates between sharing information with those who need to know, versus disclosure to the public at large.

Sharing information with those legally in a position to intervene is not treated as "privileged communication" which parents can control.

The general trend in the law is toward protection for sharing pertinent case information at all phases of the investigative process (McEvoy, 1990). In many districts, child protective service agencies are permitted to provide feedback to schools regarding the disposition of a case after the initial report is made by school personnel, especially if sharing this information is deemed to be in the best interests of the child. Such information is useful to educators as they attempt to address the special needs of these children. While schools can be liable for recklessly disclosing child abuse information to those not professionally involved in the situation, increasingly the law recognizes that sharing case information with appropriate individuals and agencies can aid intervention efforts with abused children.

Health Screening

When it comes to identifying and reporting abuse and neglect, a school nurse (when present) is an especially important member of the team. The nurse expands and enhances the team's competence by enabling its members to examine the problem from the perspectives of health and medicine. The nurse functions as the team's health appraiser and health counselor in cases where known or suspected maltreatment jeopardizes the child's ability to perform in school.

As a health appraiser, the school nurse makes observations and gathers information required in assessing the students' health status. Generally, it is through screening programs and teacher referrals that the problem of abuse or neglect is brought to attention.

Medical and dental screening of kindergarten and elementary school children is a valuable tool in detecting maltreatment. It enables the school to participate in early diagnostic and preventive measures which serve to protect children from further physical injury or neglect. If through the screening process, signs of child neglect or abuse are observed, the nurse is obligated to report these observations.

Teachers have no legal authority to conduct medical exams or to remove a child's clothing in order to examine injuries. Examination for injury falls within the nurse's domain. Moreover, in many areas school nurses or other designated persons are allowed to take photographs in order to document abuse. Educators should consult the law in their area before photographs are taken.

Staff referral is the most common avenue by which the school nurse is brought into contact with children suffering from maltreatment. If the nurse is to be an effective child advocate in the school setting, then time must be devoted to the task of public relations and to public health education. In the long run, this will be time well spent.

Of course, not all schools employ nurses. Regardless of whether there is a nurse present, all school staff should:

- become acquainted with child abuse and neglect laws and regulations;

- develop a working knowledge of their school district's child abuse and neglect policy;

- be on the alert for symptoms of child abuse and neglect;

- keep as complete and as specific a set of files recording observations of symptoms as is feasible;

- report all suspected cases of child abuse and neglect to the appropriate school official or mandated agency.

STAFF TRAINING REQUIREMENTS

At present, the majority of states and provinces do not require teacher training in child abuse and neglect, even though teachers and other staff are designated as mandated reporters. In those instances where the law demands such training, there is variation in the amount and type required. Furthermore, funding to support such training usually is inadequate or altogether nonexistent. Similarly, relatively few colleges of education which train future teachers offer required child abuse curriculum in order to be certified. In essence, the degree to which schools are legally responsible for hiring (or for failing to hire) staff trained in child abuse issues, as well as the necessary type and amount of training, has yet to be specified in the law (McEvoy, 1990).

In a few areas, mandated reporters such as teachers are required to sign a statement indicating that they are familiar with reporting laws. Yet such an approach is no substitute for proper training. To their credit, most school districts attempt to offer occasional inservice training in the area of child abuse and neglect. An ad hoc approach, however, is a far cry from a systematic and ongoing training program.

> **The sad fact remains that all too often staff training is by the method of "baptism by fire," with little more than a few printed handouts to guide their actions. A combination of lack of resources, excessive professional demands, and lack of specificity in state or provincial laws has contributed to this situation.**

Reluctance to Report

Legal and ethical demands dictate that educators report the suspicion of child maltreatment. Given limited training or knowledge about child abuse, however, some staff members may be reluctant to report their suspicions. Specifically, some staff members may:

- operate from the premise that communication between themselves and their students is confidential; if the staff learn of abuse or neglect during a private conference, they may believe it is unethical or illegal to divulge it;

- fear that they will alienate the parents if the child's injury turns out to be accidental;

- fear that they will alienate the child by violating a confidence or by "getting the parents into trouble;"

- fear that the abused student will be placed in further jeopardy if the parents learn of the referral;

- believe that it is not the school's responsibility to intervene in domestic matters, particularly in areas involving "parenting style;"

- believe that they alone can affect reasonable change in parental behavior without additional professional assistance; or

- believe that the child protective services will not effectively intervene on behalf of the child.

While these concerns are worth examining, they pale in comparison to the consequences of not providing children at risk with the services and resources of trained professionals.

> **The task of child protection is beyond the capacity of any single school employee to handle in isolation from professional protective service workers.**

One difficulty is that not all maltreated children and adolescents exhibit clear and easily documented symptoms of abuse. This lack of clear evidence understandably contributes to reluctance in reporting. One legally and ethically appropriate way for teachers and others to obtain more information is to request that special assessments be conducted. For example, a school psychologist can conduct a series of tests to determine the educational needs or deficits of a student. Given that many mistreated children exhibit learning or behavioral problems, testing is a desirable way to document problems. Following such tests, even more information can be obtained in conferences with parents regarding test results.

Some school staff may mistakenly assume that all information they gain during private conferences takes the form of "confidential or privileged communications" and is not to be divulged to any third party. We advise them to examine their state's statutes on this matter to determine their obligations under the law.

In general, the principle of confidentiality between students and school counselors is given high priority in statutes. The intent of the law is to affirm the premise that confidentiality promotes trust and acceptance between a counselor and client. And most would agree that a violation of this trust undermines effective treatment.

As previously mentioned, however, the law also recognizes that exceptions to this principle of confidentiality exist. Among the conditions under which a school counselor may divulge confidential information from a student are:

- the student's physical or mental condition requires others to assume responsibility for him or her;

- the student is in clear and immediate danger of harm from others (e.g., life is being threatened), or is in imminent danger of inflicting serious self-harm (e.g., attempting suicide);

- the student poses a clear and immediate danger to others (e.g., intends to kill parents).

In any of these situations, the school counselor is expected to report to a responsible authority or to take other emergency measures as the situation demands. The law recognizes and protects school staff for acting as any "reasonable" person would under the circumstances. In cases where the student informs a staff member that he or she has been abused, the professional is clearly in a position to reveal this information to a child protective agency, and is legally protected for filing the report.

CAN TEAMS

The CAN Team may be part of a larger crisis response team composed of professionals from various schools and agencies, or it may be formed independently. One example of how a CAN Team might function in the referral process is reflected in the following sequence:

1. Any teacher or staff member suspecting child abuse or neglect should immediately convey this information orally to the building staff person responsible for receiving referrals. This person will be the coordinator of the building child abuse and neglect team. Within a period of one working day, a written report should be made.

2. A timely meeting should be called by the principal in order for the referring staff member and the CAN Team to discuss alternatives. The purpose of the meeting is to gather and share information relevant to the child and his or her family. It is also a means to provide peer support for staff who must deal with an emotionally charged situation.

3. If deemed appropriate under the circumstances, the child should be observed in school or interviewed in private by a trained staff member. The goal is to obtain as much information from the child as possible without making the child feel uncomfortable. However, this step should not be

taken without the consultation or direction of an authorized person from the appropriate child protective services agency. If the child is willing, and if there is proper authorization, the school nurse might examine him or her **without** removing clothing covering the genital area. If the interview seems to confirm the suspicion of abuse or neglect, a report should be written immediately and submitted by the coordinator of the CAN Team.

4. The principal or other designated coordinator of the CAN Team should promptly contact the appropriate social service or law enforcement agency and request that an agency representative meet with school staff and receive a written report. In order to expedite the reporting process, the standardized reporting form of the school district should be used.

5. The coordinator of the CAN Team, or a school counselor or social worker, should be assigned to follow-up on the agency's progress in dealing with the child and his or her family. As the case develops, teachers and other relevant school staff should be given as much feedback as possible, within the bounds of the law and of professional ethics.

Although the exact composition and function of child protection teams varies, they represent an increasingly common response to the problem of child maltreatment. Such teams constitute a means by which schools can decrease the chances of error when encountering child abuse because decision making is shared, and second opinions are built into the framework of responding (Bross, 1988).

Abuse by School Staff

School responsibility for child protection is not limited to reporting suspected abuse in the home. Conditions which prove injurious to a child due to the actions of school staff raise the specter of child abuse allegations.

> **Child abuse and neglect teams must also address the possibility that school staff are implicated in child maltreatment.**

There are several paramount concerns here. For example, to what extent are schools liable if individual staff members are guilty of physically or sexually abusing students? The legal principle of "respondent superior" suggests that, under certain circumstances, agents who hire and supervise can be liable for the actions of employees. However, it is not clear how this principle applies to situations where staff clearly violate the school's stated policy by their abusive actions.

Similarly, in the context of screening applicants for staff positions, are schools liable for failure to detect a history of abusive behaviors among employees who subsequently harm children? Although schools may be liable for retaining rather than firing known abusers, are they liable for unknowingly hiring them? Does the existence of abuse by staff necessarily mean that the school has failed to provide a safe environment, especially if the abuse is undetected by school authorities? To what extent does the law protect "whistle blowers" who fear retaliation for reporting child abuse within the school system? This question is particularly important because the dual goals of child protection and protecting the school from liability, can be at odds with each other if the school attempts to suppress information as a means to avoid tort action.

At present, the laws regarding school liability have yet to be fully articulated and tested, thus providing for a variety of interpretations and responses as they evolve. Despite such ambiguities, however, it appears that schools can be held accountable in situations where school officials ignored evidence of staff abuse of children, thus allowing a risk situation to continue without taking appropriate action.

Corporal Punishment as Abuse

One question generating heated debate concerns whether a charge of child abuse can be levied against school personnel who inflict corporal punishment on students. In the United States, for example, many states currently permit the use of corporal punishment in schools. In 1988, the U.S. Department of Education reported that over a million children annually are subject to physical punishment by teachers, principals and coaches. While many national organizations oppose the use of corporal punishment (e.g., American Bar Association, National Education Association, American Psychological Association, Parent-Teachers Association to name a few), the practice continues to enjoy legal support. Moreover, the United States and Great Britain are the only industrialized countries which have failed to abandon corporal punishment in schools. While a lengthy analysis of corporal punishment is beyond the scope of this discussion, suffice it to say that legal opposition to the practice points to a lack of procedural safeguards to limit its use.

The precedent for allowing educators to employ corporal punishment for disciplinary purposes is embedded in the concept of "in loco parentis," derived from common law. This concept implies the right of educators to administer corporal punishment to children if it is deemed necessary for their proper education.

In 1977 the U.S. Supreme Court, in Ingrahm *v.* Wright, ruled in a five-to-four decision that inflicting moderate corporal punishment which is "reasonably necessary," is not a violation of constitutional rights. Specifically, this bellwether decision embodied three principles guiding schools. First, "reasonable" corporal punishment is not a violation of Eighth Amendment protection against cruel and unusual punishment. Second, the right of the state to guarantee proper discipline in the school is superior to parents' rights to determine the disciplinary methods for their children. Finally, due process concerns as applied in criminal cases, such as notice of a hearing prior to imposition of punishment, are not applicable to non-criminal penalties such as corporal punishment (Ackerman and Cohen, 1988).

Challenges to this decision have been advanced, primarily on grounds that the Supreme Court failed to distinguish between reasonable and excessive corporal punishment. In a number of instances, tort action has been directed against schools on the grounds that their use of corporal punishment was excessive and therefore an infringement upon due process rights.

For example, in 1980 the U.S. Court of Appeals for the Forth Circuit Court in Hall *v.* Tawney, ruled that the disciplinary actions taken by school officials were excessive and brutal, violating a student's due process rights. In this case, a student was punished "without apparent provocation," contrary to the express wishes of the parents, resulting in traumatic injury requiring admission to the emergency room (Reitman, 1988). Although the court found that "life and liberty" were violated by the school, the case was never appealed to the Supreme Court. However, in 1988 the Supreme Court declined to review the case of Garcia *v.* Miera, which also charged that a school's use of corporal punishment violated substantive due process, therefore making it liable for recovery of damages.

In general, child abuse laws do not appear applicable to cases of corporal punishment administered in school under appropriate guidelines. Unfortunately, the courts have failed to provide schools with specific guidelines in this area, especially with respect to distinguishing between "reasonable" and "excessive." In the absence of such guidelines, it seems likely that suits against schools will continue in cases involving significant physical injury requiring medical treatment, permanent damage, or absence from school.

One of the important tasks of the CAN Team is to review the school's policy on corporal punishment. All instances where corporal punishment has been administered should be subject to periodic review. If the school has elected to use corporal punishment on students (a practice which we do not recommend), then the CAN Team should make certain that proper safeguards are established and followed. CAN Teams should also be sensitive to the special needs of abused children who may be acting out in school.

> **Because child abuse is often a "hidden crime," employing corporal punishment can result in children who are already abused at home being subject to more physical coercion in school.**

In reviewing these practices, CAN Teams should be mindful that there is no empirical evidence that corporal punishment in schools is more effective in maintaining discipline than other methods. Indeed, the physical pain and psychological degradation associated with physically coercive means of controlling children can result in the opposite of what is intended: a rejection of authority, deep resentment of the school, and a continuation of rebellious behavior as proof of toughness. This is devastating to the learning environment.

WORKING WITH SERVICE AGENCIES

Schools are not solely responsible for working out the problems of abusive families. Educators cannot hope to meet the special needs of abuse victims without considerable support and shared information from outside the classroom. Schools are in no position to do all the necessary investigative and therapeutic work with abused children and adolescents, to the exclusion of protective service agencies. Not only is such a complex task beyond the school's sphere of competence and legal authority, but solitary efforts can make the problem worse. However well-intentioned, acting alone can result in heightened parental resistance and limited access to a range of needed interventions. A team approach, where schools and agency professionals jointly develop ameliorative strategies, has the greatest chance of success.

At least one staff member from the school should be responsible for maintaining contact with the various agencies involved. Names of contact persons in each agency encourages both referral and follow-up. Care should be taken when working with agency professionals that a message of cooperation, rather than criticism of their performance, be communicated. Make it clear that a willingness to help and work together is not meant as implied criticism. Indeed, the impression should be conveyed that the school is grateful for the assistance provided by the agency.

Although child protective agencies are responsible for conducting case investigations following a referral, school staff can be of assistance in this process. Nearly all protective service agencies have limited staff and large case loads. School staff, under the direction of protective services, could assist in providing useful background information by talking with cafeteria workers, bus drivers, coaches or others who might be in a position to see the child in another setting. Assistance can also be provided in constructing case histories by interviewing current and former teachers, as well as through the examination of school records. Conducting confidential interviews, however, should only be done under the guidance of protective services.

One of the most important contributions school staff can make is simply to volunteer their services to those legally mandated to intervene on behalf of the child. Many times school nurses, social workers, school psychologists, counselors and others can help child protective service staff in unique ways they may not have anticipated, but which prove to be invaluable to the children.

WORDS OF CAUTION

While proper reporting and referral of abuse is critical, school staff should not assume the role of being case investigators. By limiting themselves to identifying and reporting, school staff wisely avoid trying to verify on their own whether or not it is an actual case of child abuse or neglect. Verification is not the responsibility of school personnel. In this respect, school staff should not take matters into their own hands.

Contacting parents independently may only cause problems for the school and more pain to the child. Similarly, teachers or other school staff should not take an abused child to their home in order to provide temporary protection. Such well-intentioned action can place one at legal risk (e.g., being charged by parent with unlawful detention). Unless given the proper authority, or in the case of a clear health and safety emergency, school staff should not take physically abused children to a physician or hospital for treatment. The appropriate authorities should be informed so that they can take whatever action is necessary. Parental consent is generally required in such instances, and child abuse and neglect law details the limits of protection afforded professionals.

Finally, school staff members should neither delay reporting a suspected case of abuse or neglect, nor should they assume that the situation will not repeat itself. Chances are that if the child has been abused once, he or she will be abused again. If it is a first time, a report could very well save the child from further harm. Whenever a report is made, maintaining a good working relationship with child protective agencies is both legally prudent and in the best interests of the child.

8
HELPING SURVIVORS
AND THEIR PARENTS

Identifying and reporting victims of parental abuse does not end the school's responsibility to these children; educators must also learn to communicate effectively with both victims and their parents. What are the unique problems faced by teachers, school counselors, school social workers, principals, and other staff as they relate to children who are maltreated? What are the most effective ways of communicating with students in crisis? How should school personnel respond to the parents of these children? Our responses to abused children and to their abusive care givers depend, of course, on what we expect of them.

THE VICTIM: WHAT TO EXPECT

For many educators, neither their professional training nor their personal backgrounds adequately prepare them for encounters with abused children and teenagers. In order to provide them with help, educators need to consider how abuse victims learn to cope and how they construct a world view.

It is common among victims of physical or sexual abuse to have feelings of fear, distrust, rejection, guilt, anger, low self-esteem and a pervasive sense of powerlessness. These children may isolate themselves from others as a means of avoiding conflicts. They may have learned that it is best not to trust anyone, and hence they do not seek assistance for themselves. They may have been ordered by parents never to talk to anyone about what goes on at home. Many of these victims have never learned to develop healthy and nurturing relationships with others. In short, many of the competencies one might take for granted in others, are underdeveloped or absent in these children. When encountering abused children and teenagers, educators should keep in mind the following:

- Do not expect victims of parental exploitation to automatically hate their abusive parents. Most victims love their parents, although they may resent how their parents are treating them.

- Anticipate that maltreated children and adolescents will want to protect their parents. These children are very fearful of "causing" their families to break-up or of their parents going to jail. Children frequently deny being abused out of loyalty or fear of being blamed for causing their families trouble.

- Because abusive parents are often experts at denial, anticipate that children who exhibit symptoms of abuse or neglect may not define themselves as victims. Many abused children learn to accept their parents' view of events, and believe that they cause their parents to harm them. Indeed, many victims of prolonged maltreatment may believe that their home situation is normal and hence, do not fully recognize what is happening.

- Expect that victims of parental abuse will have a difficult time trusting adults. Being harmed by a parent constitutes a "core experience" wherein fear, distrust and withdrawal are a means of coping with a fundamental contradiction: their protectors are harming them. As such, they may believe that no one can be trusted, including those seeking to help them.

- Do not expect or encourage abused children to feel a debt of gratitude for your assistance. Many abused children have such limited communication skills that they do not know how to express thanks when help is offered. Furthermore, feelings of indebtedness can turn to resentment if the help giver expects recognition for the help given. Many youth in need, especially teenagers, will refuse assistance in order to avoid feeling indebted.

- Do not expect "miracle cures." Victims of abuse often have experienced a pattern of maltreatment extending over months or years. As such, they may have developed ways of coping which are troubling to you (e.g., denial, acting out, withdrawal). Therefore do not be discouraged if efforts to help fail to meet with immediate success.

- Do not expect all abused children to be the same or to have identical needs. No single approach is applicable to all. One's relationship with an abused child should develop naturally without seeming contrived or forced. Being patient, empathic and honest with children nearly always is a precondition for successful intervention.

- Do not force decisions on abused children or teenagers, unless there is a compelling health or safety concern. Abuse victims need to gain a sense of power and control over their lives. Imposing decisions upon them tends to reinforce feelings of powerlessness.

HOW TO HELP

Educators should not try to be professional "therapists" with abused students. Similarly, it is not the responsibility of the school to become directly involved in rehabilitating abusive parents. Rather, the form of help educators can offer maltreated children is indirect.

One way educators can help abused children is to provide solace through increased knowledge. Even though this will not resolve problematic situations at home, raising questions and providing facts about abusive interaction can be an important palliative for those who are victimized.

Realistic classroom discussions about family violence, alcoholism, sexual abuse and other problems will provide victims with a context to assess these conditions in their lives, and to consider possible courses of action.

Classroom discussions also provide an opportunity for victims to express themselves under circumstances where they are likely to receive support. Talking about feelings and experiences in a supportive environment affords students perspective, as well as the opportunity to gain insight from the experiences of others. Many will discover that the confusion they feel is normal given the circumstances of their lives, and that others have endured similar traumas.

Classroom discussions can also function to identify youth who would benefit most from interventions. By the way they respond, educators can observe students who may be experiencing physical or emotional risks due to conditions at home. It is therefore important to create an atmosphere of openness in school wherein students feel comfortable in talking about personal troubles or the problems they have observed in others.

> **Presenting factual information in a manner which encourages honest responses can open the door to situations in their lives that have been "taboo," while serving as a means of identifying needs and initiating appropriate intervention.**

Develop Trusting Relationships

Teachers and other school staff should do all they can to provide the kind of support system where abused children feel that they can discuss their problems. Initially, abused children may feel shame, embarrassment and guilt about their family life. They may be reluctant to express any of their feelings openly. Perhaps an abused child has been ordered by his or her parents to remain silent. When this occurs, educators should not pressure the child to self-disclose. Rather, by showing empathy and a willingness to listen without being critical, the child may eventually express pent-up feelings. Such self-disclosure is an important step in coming to terms with deep-seated fears and a poor self-image.

Much of what abused children and teenagers divulge about their lives is shocking and disturbing. A technique for helping students to talk about their problems is to ask them "how" and "what" questions rather than "why" questions. Questions such as "Why did you do that?" or "Why didn't you try this?" make victims feel the need to defend rather than express their feelings. Placing them in a defensive posture usually results in restricted and ineffective communication. A better approach is to ask questions such as "How did you feel about it?" or "What were you thinking at the time?" The point is that abuse victims are more willing to express themselves, and are more open to receiving help, when they feel they are not being judged. Regardless of how upsetting the situation may be, remember to approach abused children with a sense of warmth and understanding without judging them.

All school staff should keep in mind certain rules of thumb when questioning students who are maltreated. Remember that it is common for those who are victimized at home to feel a deep sense of shame and embarrassment. Many have never spoken to anyone about what happened or about how they feel. Educators should avoid violating their privacy by "interrogating" them. Letting victims decide the content of the discussion gives them the opportunity to gain control over their feelings. Also keep in mind that victimized children and adolescents seldom want pity. Discussions with them should be open, sincere and friendly, without being overly sympathetic to the point of pity.

In learning of maltreatment, it is not the educator's responsibility to determine whether the abuse was intentional or to identify the conditions surrounding the incident. Such probing can be traumatic for the student and is best conducted within the professional bounds of case work. Likewise, school staff should not call or visit a child's parents or relatives when questions of abuse or neglect arise, unless under the specific direction of protective agency staff.

Most abused children and adolescents see themselves as lacking the ability to alter the conditions of their lives. They feel powerless. Involving them in making decisions about school matters, even seemingly insignificant decisions, can help them to gain a sense of control. While it is useful to point out options and to help the students consider the ramifications of various courses of action, making decisions for them usually is not the best tactic.

> **A feeling of autonomy is usually a necessary condition for the victim of abuse to mobilize his or her own resources to overcome problems.**

Finally, pay special attention to recurring themes abused children raise in their conversations or exhibit in their school work (e.g., sexual or violent themes). These are clues providing insight into especially troubling areas for these children. Such knowledge is useful in guiding decisions about counseling and developing effective approaches to instruction.

Crisis Communication

If a student reveals abuse to a teacher or other staff member, it is an indication of trust and a way of asking for help. Oftentimes such a revelation occurs at a time when the student is near the "breaking point." This means that the crisis in his or her life may have escalated to the point where serious action such as running away or suicide is contemplated. This is especially true if the victim is an adolescent. In order to communicate effectively with students in crisis, educators should do the following:

- Realize your own limitations. Working with abused students is challenging, but emotionally draining. Do not be afraid to ask for help before your emotional reserves are depleted.

- Refrain from trivializing the student's problems by indicating that he or she is "overreacting." What seems like a small matter to an adult can be momentous to a young person. Failure to acknowledge the validity of a student's feelings or problems reduces open communication.

- Avoid the tendency to respond by being judgmental or moralizing about a student's feelings or behavior (e.g. "You shouldn't feel that way."). Such reactions tend to convey a message of rejection.

- Never suggest that the student was physically or sexually abused because she or he did something wrong (e.g., acted provocatively).

- Do not apply "reverse psychology" on a student who is threatening to run away or to take other drastic action. Challenging a student to "go ahead and do it" may be the deciding factor which compels him or her to make good on a threat.

- Resist the urge to take sides against family members. Even when family members are abusive, reinforcing the view that they are villains may make the troubled youth feel even more alone.

- Communicate the view to abused children that their crisis or pain is temporary, that help is available to solve their problems, and that you are willing to stand by them until their problems are resolved.

- Do not validate feelings of hopelessness or helplessness. Rather, convey empathy but emphasize the positive things one can do to gain control.

Be a Role Model

It may sound glib, but perhaps the best way to build trust among abused students is by being a proper role model for **all** students. Being a good role model implies several things. First, it means that one behaves in a consistent and fair way. To show favoritism toward some, or to publicly single out others as "problem kids," may reinforce feelings of distrust and hostility. As a role model, it is especially important to develop an attitude of respect for the rights of others — a guiding ethic which communicates that *"I will not use others for my ends, without concern for their needs."*

Among the most effective role models in school are those persons who are willing to take the risk of trusting students, even though they will at times be disappointed. Being trusted implies a responsibility to respond in kind to the person who is trusting.

Unfortunately, all too often those who could be good role models for students lose this advantage by routinely communicating messages of distrust toward all.   When this is done, the distrust becomes mutual, further isolating students who are at risk from adult support.

Being an effective role model also means that one should not expect students to automatically submit to one's presumed authority.   Oftentimes adults feel that because they have good intentions toward students, their authority and credibility should not be challenged.   Children and adolescents who have been victimized, as well as those who have not been abused, may not accept without question the authority of adults.   Becoming a credible authority usually occurs gradually. If one demonstrates the qualities of empathy, trust, acceptance, consistency and competence, trust will develop.   Demanding submission only serves to reinforce feelings of powerlessness and distrust.

Finally, being a supportive role model means that one must be ready to "put up or shut up" if a victim of abuse is willing to be helped. It is easy to glibly offer help if one does not believe the offer will be accepted. Empty gestures are worse than doing nothing at all. Insincerity when offering help only reinforces in victims the belief that their mistrust is well-founded and that they truly are alone. Often the most sincere form of help is simply a willingness to participate in normal activities with the student such as talk or play. It also means that one is ready to give time on another's terms, rather than strictly on one's own.

Foster Positive Peer Relations

One effective way to help abused children is to surround them with positive and supportive people. For maltreated children who have not developed healthy relationships with adults, the nature of their peer relationships is extremely important. School-related extracurricular activities represent one area in which educators can foster positive peer relationships.

Involving victims in school activities which result in praise and in opportunities to make decisions can reduce low self-esteem, feelings of powerlessness, lack of trust, and feelings of isolation. A victim's feelings of worthlessness also are reduced when he or she experiences a sense of accomplishment and belonging, perhaps through the cooperative actions of teams, clubs, or informal groups. While extending an abused child's network of peer affiliation may not stop parental maltreatment, it does help to reduce his or her isolation by establishing meaningful relations with others.

> **Cooperative learning exercises in the classroom also can increase an abused child's positive interaction with peers and adults.**

Peer Assistance Programs

Many schools in the United States and Canada have developed peer assistance or peer helpers programs. These programs are designed to use trained student leaders to help their peers. Students are trained to serve as listeners, discussion leaders, tutors and support persons available to their peers on and off the school premises. This approach recognizes that students who are having problems often turn to their peers for help, rather than first seeking the assistance of an adult.

Peer assistance programs are a valuable means of identifying problems which might escape the notice of adults. While not intended to serve as a substitute for professional counseling, peer assistance programs are an important adjunct to a school's efforts at intervention and referral. In relying upon an already existing system of peer-to-peer interaction, abused students who might otherwise fall through the cracks can be identified, referred and given needed support (McEvoy, 1990).

Individual Instruction with Caution

Being a victim of physical, sexual, or psychological abuse can seriously inhibit a student's development and school performance. Listlessness, poor attention span, inability to work autonomously or to retain information, or any other number of problems are common. In order to overcome learning problems, educators may wish to consider developing individual study plans tailored to the special educational needs of each maltreated child.

An individualized program has the greatest chance of being successful if the classroom teacher can organize and implement it in light of detailed information concerning the unique conditions of the student's family. It is imperative that the person responsible for compiling casework information keep teachers and other appropriate school staff informed. Likewise, school staff should not hesitate to make frequent inquiries to the person doing follow-up work on each case. Continual contact with the case is the best way to foster understanding of each student's special needs.

Once teachers and other school staff have the necessary information to develop an individualized program, they should be mindful of the manner in which this program is presented. Teachers should avoid at all costs anything which publicly calls attention to a student's abusive home. Any special assistance should appear to all students as a natural part of the curriculum.

Educators should not focus attention on the maltreated child in such a way as to make other students feel ignored or offended. All too often in human relationships we unwittingly hurt or anger one person by trying to reassure and help another. The goal is to establish supportive adult relationships and instructional plans without creating estrangements. Such efforts make sense with all students but are especially important when working with abuse victims.

> **Educators who work with a maltreated student should avoid conveying the impression that the child's parents are inadequate or unloving. Never be openly critical of parents in front of students.**

Educators should make a conscious effort to avoid conferring upon abused children or their parents a "deviant" label. Similarly, teachers and other school staff should not be overly critical of abused children who are poor academic achievers. Criticism from educators can add unnecessary pressure to an abused student's home situation, thus provoking even more maltreatment. Whenever progress reports are given to parents, they should include positive information as well as specific ways to improve or remediate any weakness.

RELATING TO ABUSIVE PARENTS

Many professionals recognize that one key to successfully addressing the problem of child maltreatment is to offer programming directly to abusive parents. Special programs for these parents should be conducted by community agencies under the direct control of protective services. Although it is not the responsibility of schools to change the behavior of abusive parents, often school social workers, school psychologists, and even teachers are called upon to help community agencies who do work with these parents. Because educators and agency staff alike benefit from a close working relationship, it is important for all to understand when interventions with parents are likely to improve how they behave toward their children.

Unfortunately, the task of altering parenting behaviors among chronic abusers has proven to be difficult. Part of the difficulty resides in the differing characteristics and agendas abusive parents bring to the educational or therapeutic setting. For example, the reasons for abusive parents to receive help can range from a desire to manage the impressions of case workers and school officials, to a genuine desire to change. What, then, determines the likelihood that programming (including therapy) for abusive parents will be successful? When is it likely to produce little or no change in parents? What should educators, therapists, case workers, school psychologists and others working with these parents be alert to in assessing those most and least likely to benefit from interventions?

While there is considerable variation among parents who mistreat their children, research does point to several patterns which impact on the relative success of interventions with these parents. Specifically, abusive parents are least likely to be candidates for successful intervention programming the more they are characterized by the following:

- Parent has history of severe abuse as a child or regularly observed extreme violence between parents.

- Parent is in program only because of a court mandate, and is deeply resentful of that mandate.

- Parent has extensive prior record of being a child abuser, and past interventions have failed to alter the abuse pattern.

- Parent has no support network to provide emotional, material or other assistance in times of stress.

- Parent is experiencing a high level of chronic stress and depression (e.g., is unemployed or underemployed, is in the process of a divorce or undergoing severe marital discord).

- Parent exhibits chronic pattern of alcohol or drug abuse.

- Parent shows signs of a deteriorating mental condition (e.g., psychotic, persistent paranoia, severe character disorder).

- Parental abuse of children is associated with compulsive and freakish or bizarre rituals.

- Parent persists in denying abuse despite clear evidence to the contrary.

- Parental verbalizations and behaviors suggest a decided dislike or resentment of the child, or of the person(s) attempting to teach appropriate parenting skills.

- Parental communication skills are very limited and do not appear to be improving with programming (e.g., parent is bored, inattentive, refuses to listen or take suggestions, is unwilling to self-disclose or cannot articulate even the most rudimentary feelings).

- During and following intervention program, monitoring of parental behavior by appropriate agencies is inadequate or non-existent.

On the other hand, the prospects for improving parenting behaviors among abusers are enhanced when the parent is characterized by the following:

- Parent assumes responsibility for actions and does not engage in denial.

- Parent exhibits good communication skills, listens and is willing to self-disclose.

- Parent is not abusing alcohol or other drugs.

- Parent has access to a network of support to help him or her in time of need.

- Parent has entered program voluntarily out of a sincere desire to change.

- Stress levels in the parent's environment are low and situational rather than extreme and chronic, and the parent shows no symptoms of deteriorating mental condition.

- Parent shows genuine empathy for child and an awareness of the child's needs.

- Monitoring or follow-up of parent continues after he or she completes the program.

Although treating abusive parents is not the responsibility of schools, educators inevitably will be in contact with these parents regarding their children's conduct in school. Educators should realize that they have a role to play with abusive parents, whether they like it or not.

How teachers interact with students in the classroom or on the playground, the assignments they make, and the substance of what they teach combine to affect the interactions between students and their parents. In parent-teacher conferences, for example, what otherwise might be considered appropriate information given to parents in order to help children, may make matters worse in the case of abusive homes. Special care is needed when educators relate to abusive parents in the context of parent-teacher conferences or other routine communications between the school and the home.

Maintain Emotional Control

Abusive parents need reassurance and the opportunity to feel good about themselves if they are to stop being abusive. Therefore, the initial step all educators must take is to come to terms with their own feelings about child maltreatment. The proper professional stance concerning maltreated children and their parents should be one of objectivity. School staff should never convey a sense of admonition or moral revulsion to the parents. If anything, they should attempt to convey a feeling of understanding and support with respect to the difficulties of parenting, without condoning the abuse. This is especially important if the parents are already feeling isolated or hostile.

Avoid Being Adversarial

When abuse is discovered, parents often become very defensive and hostile toward "outsiders" they perceive to be judgmental. Because educators have such close contact with children, abusive parents may be especially hostile and defensive during encounters with school staff.

> Educators should be on guard not to be placed in the role of adversary. Regardless of their feelings, school staff (especially teachers) should be careful not to convey to parents a message of condemnation. Good rapport with these parents can only serve to help their children.

Unless specifically directed to do so by protective agency staff or as part of a parenting program, educators should not offer gratuitous advice to abusive parents on how to be good parents. Well-intentioned but unsolicited advice is likely to be viewed with suspicion and hostility by the parent, especially if that advice is perceived to have little to do with the child's school-related functioning. The prudent course is for school staff to keep their discussions limited to questions of the child's school activity. If asked, however, educators can help parents by suggesting effective parenting literature, or by directing them to classes and workshops in the community which are designed to improve parenting skills. Such classes are open to abusive and non-abusive parents alike, and therefore are not likely to stigmatize those who attend.

Do Not Assume Guilt

Educators should be cautious in making assumptions about a parent who is presumed to be abusive, especially if an investigation has not been completed. For example, it is not uncommon for disaffected spouses to publicly accuse each other of child abuse in order to gain an advantage in custody battles.

> **Educators should be alert to the possibility of a false accusation of abuse, especially if the claim is made by a parent who is in the process of a bitter divorce.**

Being labeled an abuser carries considerable social stigma which has implications for a person's future career and home life. Unless a case of abuse has been confirmed by legally authorized professionals, school staff should be careful in drawing conclusions without proof. The specter of a false accusation should reinforce the importance of close cooperation and communication between agency professionals and educators.

Respect Confidentiality

It is important to remind all school staff about the rights of parents and children to confidentiality. Instances of child abuse and neglect may seem like interesting topics for coffee room discussions or out of school conversations. However, divulging information about a student's family life should be done only under legally and ethically proper circumstances. A student's classmates, neighbors, school volunteers and other non-authorized persons should not have access to such privy information. Rumors which impugn the reputation of a family (even if the rumors are true) may function to further isolate that family from needed help and retard the success of therapeutic efforts.

Avoid Issuing Warnings

Teachers and other school staff may believe that they can prevent further abuse by warning a family that a report will be made if the abuse or neglect continues. Such action is seldom effective and can place the child at greater risk. Protective agency staff are trained in interviewing techniques and case investigation; they alone are legally and professionally equipped to intervene. In this regard, the educator's primary responsibility is to call attention to suspected cases and to maintain contact with those doing the casework.

In designing interventions for maltreated children and their parents, one question should always guide the actions of those providing help: Will this intervention improve the mental, physical, and social competencies of the child? Scarce resources should be devoted only to those interventions which work to build such competencies.

Part C
Primary
Prevention

9
PREPARATION FOR ADULTHOOD

Reducing the emergence of child maltreatment in the first instance — not merely responding to abuse after it occurs — is our best hope. It is almost certain, given the current growth in child maltreatment, that the problem will become even more unmanageable unless we do something soon to change three conditions. We must:

- alter mistaken ideas that permeate much of our culture about what is tolerable for children;

- reduce the severe impairments in knowledge and skills that characterize a growing number of people who are potential but not yet abusers; and

- subdue the estrangement values of self-centeredness whereby individuals place their own gratification ahead of even their own children.

How do we produce a shift toward increasing the proportion of healthy parents in our society? The task seems complex and there are many institutions with influence. As a society we have families, religious organizations, schools, economic conditions, and the media, each having an impact on how parents treat their children. Clearly, our social institutions influence the character of family life.

Can we expect any of these institutions to change what family members are doing? As a society, if we conclude that there is nothing any institution can do, or if we say that no institution has the right to teach all individuals ethical and humane ways of living together, then child abuse will increase. Child abuse will increase along with its growing contribution to more crime and violence in society.

If we conclude that we can make a difference, then perhaps we have a chance. But to which institutions do we direct our expectations and resources for instilling knowledge, skills and values for healthy parenting? What institution is in a position to directly enter into the lives of millions of people who have not yet harmed children?

Certainly we cannot expect "healthy" parents to diagnose, identify and then go into the homes of those other millions of "less healthy" families and impose upon them their values and habits. They do not have the skill or the legal capabilities for this task. We should be thankful for those who do well by their children, and we should seek their assistance for ways they can support a more humane society; but they are not up to the task of imposing their values on other families. They can, however, lead by example and by creating new mores of respect for children.

Neither can we place a demand on our religious institutions to change the values and behaviors of millions of potential abusers who do not abide by their theology. We cannot require churches, temples or mosques to impose parenting instruction upon non-members of their congregations. The best we can hope from our religious institutions, like we can hope from healthy parents, is that they reinforce healthy parenting, and be a part of the public movement which challenges violence and abuse.

As to our economic or law enforcement systems, there can be antidiscrimination, antiviolence and antiabuse laws which challenge abuse after it happens in work settings, schools, homes or elsewhere. But what can law enforcement do to change the values and beliefs in families where abuse has not yet occurred? Here the task is much more difficult.

> **It is easier for law enforcement to address the problem of abuse after it occurs than to prevent this crime in the first place.**

In other words, the legal side of government has largely restricted itself to imposing restraints or assistance after the fact of abuse. And there is no clear evidence that since 1974, when federal child abuse legislation went into effect, that our child protection efforts have impeded the growing trend in child abuse. Surely, legislation and accompanying child protection services have helped victims and abusers, but the number of victims keeps increasing. The number of child abusers appears to be increasing faster than abuse survivors are being helped.

Like our family, religious, and economic institutions, law enforcement can make a difference *after the fact* with limited numbers of parents. But if we seek to foster the promotion of healthy values in *all* citizens, collectively and politically, we must turn to the one institution that has as its mandate the training and socialization of *all* citizens — the educational system.

Fortunately, we as educators can do much, if not all that is necessary. We can instill in a larger portion of our culture knowledge about healthy human development, stronger senses of self-worth, greater competencies for addressing relationship problems, and the value to self of doing right by one's children. As educators, we can do much in spite of those facets of the mass media which glorify violence and exploitation, and in spite of the many abusers who serve as models for negative parenting with their children.

As a public institution, our educational system can teach healthy behaviors to many of our young if given certain resources and support. Then not so many of our young will in turn abuse their children when and if they become parents. This is a long-term goal, but it is the only way to reduce the trend of more violence and exploitation in our families.

Clearly, this task is central to education's mandate of producing good citizens. In this sense, the kind of primary child abuse prevention suggested here is a normal part of the educational mission of our schools; it is linked to contributing to public health and to good citizenship. The schools are in a position to reach nearly every youngster and teach factual information about living healthy lives. The schools are in a position to reach nearly every youngster and instill or reinforce self-esteem and competencies for participation in society. And only the school can reach nearly every youngster to instill or reinforce values of altruism and respect for the integrity of others.

> **In the most fundamental sense, orchestrating the education of students so they learn to respect themselves and others, including their families, amounts to an educational program for the primary prevention of child abuse.**

In the school setting, teaching this respect for others can be best accomplished in many ways, including having staff members serve as non-violent and nurturing role models. It also means that teachers, coaches, counselors, administrators, and other staff intentionally and unintentionally instruct students in what it means to do the right thing by others.

However, no one class or several classes on parenting or child abuse will be sufficient to produce parents who are healthy in their relationships with their families; certainly occasional sessions on child abuse by staff or outsiders won't do the job. Such sessions may dramatize the problem of child abuse, but they will do little to inculcate the critical values of respect for human dignity. What is needed is a coordinated and integrated curriculum that addresses citizenship at all levels.

CURRICULUM INTEGRATION

Our position is that the focus should not be on child abuse *per se*. Rather, our emphasis should be on helping students to learn about healthy ways of raising children; and this attention should be a part of the regular curriculum from preschool through high school. We should not limit the dissemination of information on parenting to one or a few elective courses. A course in "family living," sometimes called by the older name of "home economics," is a case in point. This elective course reaches only a fraction of the students, most of whom are female. Males need to learn healthy parenting skills and attitudes as much as females.

In addition, it is unfortunate that some schools use family living courses as "dumping grounds" for so called "lower track" students. This communicates that the course content is of marginal value. Nothing is further from the truth. Well taught family living courses are worthy of any college-bound or general program. They need not be watered down courses merely because they deal with matters of human relationships. Certainly, understanding human development, the relevance of various forms of social life, and the responsibilities for living in a sane society are of value to us all.

Even if students do enroll in such "family living" courses, however, they are typically offered too late to be of much value for instilling attitudes and social skills unless a proper education has been in place throughout the system for many years. Waiting until students are in high school before teaching them about the rights and obligations of responsible parenting is simply too late. By then, essential values and beliefs affecting one's life are already strongly rooted.

All students should begin to learn about healthy family life early in elementary school and continue this learning through high school, regardless of their backgrounds. Also, the emphasis should be on the positive side, talking about the advantages of nonviolence, and not centering upon abuse.

To use a medical analogy, effective instruction about human development, including child abuse, provides early "inoculation" with follow-up "booster shots" all the way through school. It is better to approach the topic of child abuse in a gradual, unobtrusive but steady manner, rather than in large but sporadic doses.

By starting early and continuing throughout the school years, the critical ideas and values about how we all should treat others, including our children, are taught and consistently reinforced.

In addition, temporary and dramatic publicity campaigns about what one is doing in sessions on child abuse do little to build a solid knowledge, skill, or motivational base for preventing either child abuse or neglect. In fact, hyped-up special public relations events on child abuse can make matters worse. Such sessions may create the illusion that a comprehensive program for teaching appropriate parenting is in place, and thereby cause the staff and the community to ignore their responsibility.

Curriculum Objectives

In developing an integrated abuse prevention curriculum, it is critical that all of the teachers in a school, along with the principal representing community orientations, play a major role in what should be taught. In the final analysis, it is the teachers, as a group, who will determine whether a program for instilling values and skills is successfully implemented; and as a group, they must "buy into" the objectives. Once this occurs, then staff-based management is critical.

Teacher-based Management. Collectively a teacher-based management approach gives the classroom teachers in a building major responsibility for determining *how* to teach in their classes the values, skills and knowledge necessary for desirable citizenship and parenting. Restated, *basic child abuse prevention in the classroom is a primary responsibility of the regular teaching staff through their teaching and modeling decency in human conduct.* An integrated teacher management approach to basic prevention places the responsibility on classroom teachers and other staff to instruct students within the context of the regular curriculum. This should be done in accord with the policies set down by the community and amplified by the school administration.

Support staff such as counselors or outside experts may assist teachers in this task, but it is the teachers who must remain in charge of their classrooms. Support staff or experts from the community should never supplant teachers in providing primary prevention instruction. They may, however, play an adjunct role when asked by teachers, or they may provide information or training to teachers.

When new concepts and program innovations are to be considered, most teachers will look with favor upon those who can help them with ideas and resources, especially if offered in a non-arrogant way. One way to begin is to create an Instructional Resource Committee and have them learn about the resources their community offers.

The same can be said for school counselors, psychologists and social workers as the curriculum involves them (for example, in conducting a peer assistance program to reduce date rape, or other problems). They should be empowered to remain in charge, but under the guidelines of the committee.

An Instructional Resource Committee. An Instructional Resource Committee should be part of the permanent, general curriculum committee structure of each school building. It should be made up mostly of teachers, plus the professional school support staff (including counselors, nurses, social workers, psychologists, and building administrators). This committee, unlike a CAN Team which provides direct help to abused children, is concerned with educating *all* students to respect the rights and integrity of others.

This permanent committee will begin to be effective when it affirmatively answers the following questions.

- Is the committee receiving input from all relevant areas in the school and the community? Does it communicate this information and other relevant findings to building staff, district personnel, and all others who should know?

- Is each class which intends to teach citizenship, including good parenting, given careful consideration to see how information fostering good citizenship is to be presented?

- Does the committee provide parents and school officials with suggested curriculum materials, goals and objectives, and other details *prior* to working with the staff or students?

- Does this committee carefully target a variety of areas of instruction rather than suggesting that any single course can instill basic values?

- Are those activities addressing citizenship and parenting which are to be conducted outside the classroom congruent with other curriculum policies?

- Is the program linked to community education efforts? Collaboration with parent-teacher organizations, with parent education projects, and with community groups working to prevent child abuse is important. Given their importance, are community workers invited to provide input?

- Is the committee assured that the students are being exposed to healthy adult role models? Through films, guest speakers, role playing, observing child care, and classroom discussions, desirable parenting should be brought into focus.

- Are students taught about the community sources which are available for helping both abusers and victims?

- Are all offerings developmentally appropriate? It should be obvious that what is offered in kindergarten should not take the same form as what is offered in subsequent years. The same can be said for offerings to those who are mentally impaired and to those who are cognitively gifted.

- Does the committee assist teachers by locating needed materials and arranging for inservice in their use.

- Are there procedures for an ongoing and useful evaluation of all phases of the program?

Instructional Content

Generally, we have said that the core values, knowledge and skills relevant to the basic prevention of child maltreatment may not explicitly address the topic of abuse. They deal with sharing, fairness, respecting others' rights, kindness and honesty. Yet by teaching students about the valid ways of treating others, one is also teaching them what is not worthy. In other words, information about child maltreatment is taught even when the topic emphasizes what is right and good.

The question then arises: When can one teach about abuse *per se?* Here careful consideration should be given to student development levels. At the early levels, one should concentrate on what is good, rather than on horrible examples of parenting. At later levels it becomes easier to explicitly treat examples of abuse. The most important point to remember in considering content is to avoid reinforcing, in any way, that abusing or neglecting children is acceptable.

In clarifying what should be covered at any particular level, answers of *yes* to the following questions seem appropriate.

- Can the suggested materials be integrated in an unobtrusive manner into the rest of the curriculum and be taught by regular classroom teachers?

- Are there materials available which are appropriate for students of all developmental levels?

- Have the teachers been given adequate training to be able to use the materials?

- Is the content designed and presented in such a way that knowledge and skills are reinforced outside the classroom (e.g., with peers and at home)?

- Will the students be afforded the opportunity to privately discuss their questions, concerns and experiences with their teachers, counselors or other professionals (if needed)?

- Does the content include not only information about assault from strangers, but also information on the more frequently occurring assault from persons known to the child?

- Is the content integrated and reinforced throughout the different grades, with the long-term goal of preparing children to become healthy adults?

Preparation at the Secondary Level

We have emphasized that all students need to be prepared for the responsibilities of marriage and parenthood. This includes educating them (especially those in high school) in the practical aspects of raising children. Topics of relevance should include child management techniques and basic child care such as how to feed and change an infant. Students should also learn about physical and cognitive development in infants and children, particularly so that they do not treat infants and young children as if they are adults. One of the basic correlates of parental abuse is parents having unrealistic expectations for their children.

As we suggest elsewhere, our high schools can provide parenting instruction by exposing students to a school-based day care program. Many now offer child day care to teenage parents who are students as a means of encouraging them to stay in school. These programs benefit other students as well. Students who work as volunteers or for credit, and who observe youngsters in child care, learn a great deal that will be valuable to them as parents.

High school students also should be encouraged to volunteer at community day care or preschool centers. Such volunteerism not only provides practical experience in child management, it provides a service to the community. Volunteering is a fine way of fostering responsible citizenship. It reinforces a core respect for what society needs in its people. Students learn about responsibilities and they learn about reality.

As observers often attest, many teenagers hold idyllic but false views of marriage and family. They fail to understand the rights and obligations of parenting. Many falsely believe that having a baby will remedy their problems with their partners. Many want a child to compensate for feelings of not being loved or of loneliness, or as a means of escaping from home. These and similarly dysfunctional attitudes and stresses set the stage for abuse and neglect.

In order to become effective at parenting, all students should learn how to cope with family stresses and conflicts, how to communicate more effectively, and how to relate to others in their families in non-exploitive ways. They need to know how to appropriately express their emotions, solve their problems, and how to assess the consequences of their actions.

Another important objective is to teach all students how to recognize a potentially violent situation and to empower them with the skills and values which may reduce the likelihood of violence. They need to learn where to find help and how to ask for help if they or others in their family are being harmed.

> **Perhaps most important, all students need to learn that child rearing tasks should not be differentiated strictly on the basis of the sex of the parent, that parental role responsibilities should be mutually agreed upon and shared, and that in households where there is a sense of equality and respect between parents, the likelihood of exploitation of children is greatly reduced.**

Inservice and Preservice Education

If our youth are to grow up and be healthy parents, then we as a group need to be much better informed about the character of child abuse and neglect than the public we serve. It is a sad commentary that many educators only learn about abuse from inservice programs, or worse, from portrayals in the mass media. However, until our colleges of education can catch up with their obligation to provide training relevant to child abuse, inservice programs will continue to be essential.

There are those who believe that the states or provinces should pass statutes mandating that all teachers be required to undergo inservice training in child abuse. Others contend that if school accreditation were contingent upon developing a curriculum which addresses abuse and neglect, then school personnel would receive better inservice about how to instruct their students.

We favor the latter but we do not advocate adding to government bureaucracies to achieve this goal. We believe that institutional resource committees in school, by the force of the evidence and if given the time, will provide a scope and sequence curriculum. Such a scope and sequence plan would detail the what, when and how core values and skills should be taught.

The low cost way of upgrading the training of teachers, of course, is to encourage colleges of education to provide more complete instruction in child development which includes the nature and consequences of abuse, as well as preventative measures, as a normal part of their psychology, methods, social foundation and practicum courses. Unfortunately, even today, most educational psychology books required in teacher education classes, merely have a tacked on chapter about child abuse. Typically, this addresses little more than incidence and symptoms of abuse. And even this much is of recent origin. Clearly there is room for improvement.

COMMUNITY EDUCATION

Adult education should also be a part of an integrated effort to reduce child abuse. In this regard, instruction for coping with family problems should be available to all adults. Fortunately, in most communities, the schools attempt to provide some training in parenting. Sometimes this involves collaboration between the school and community agencies. Sometimes social welfare agencies offer this service alone. Parenting education, however, is typically offered solely by the schools through their community education divisions. They usually offer classes at night after regular school hours when most parents can attend.

Whoever teaches parent education should include information on human development and child management values and techniques. This should be the case regardless of whether the course is designed to focus on home teaching techniques in reading, mathematics or other academic areas, how to deal with sex education in the home, how to help children cope with inappropriate peer pressures, reducing aggression between siblings, or helping children to behave properly without resorting to extreme corporal punishment. The point is that while many different parenting courses are needed to serve a variety of needs, they should all help to instill critical core values, a basic knowledge of human development and skill in child management techniques.

In every course, for example, parents need to learn that frequent or exclusive use of corporal punishment is reactive and confrontational; it often has undesirable outcomes for themselves and their offspring. They need to learn that effective child management can be accomplished without resorting to physical or verbal violence.

Parents with Special Needs Children. Recent reviews of the research literature indicate that abuse victims tend to include an exceptionally high number of children with developmental disabilities (Bartlette, 1992). What is the reason for this correlation?

There is no doubt that disabled children require much more of their parents than do other children. The financial demands, emotional energy, time and social costs of having a disabled child are considerable. If a child is viewed by parents as taking away from other loved ones, resentment can emerge. If a child is viewed as unacceptable, or too difficult to care for, or if the task of parenting is seen as becoming even more demanding, abuse may result. If a parent has an impaired child who emits behavioral patterns that are very annoying (e.g., neurologically impaired children are often characterized by chronic high pitched screaming), then again the risk of child abuse is increased. The list of conditions that make it difficult for both disabled children and their parents goes on and on; thus it is easy to see that it takes especially capable, resourceful and loving parents of impaired children to avoid being abusive without some sort of assistance.

The relationship of disability to parental abuse, however, is far more complicated than can be understood by taking into account the severity of a child's impairment. First of all not every child with a disability, not even most impaired children, are abused by their parents. The overwhelming majority of children with disabilities elicit extensive nurturance and attention from their parents. In addition, it is not the most seriously impaired, but the marginally impaired children who are at greatest risk of being abused (Bartlette, 1992).

Probably the reason for the greater risk being associated with the more moderately impaired, is that children with severe disabilities are recognized as such at birth by their parents and by various authorities. They in turn arrange for economic, health or educational assistance which lowers the risk of abuse. A related suggestion is that parental expectations for mildly impaired children tend to be exaggerated because no disability or other acceptable reason for poor performance is apparent (Bartlette, 1992).

Whatever the reason, many parents of children with mild disabilities need assistance in being "realistic" in raising their children. In school this means that the educators' role must be expanded to serve parents of mildly impaired children, even those parents who do not have children in special education classrooms.

Fortunately, our public schools already have professionals with the requisite skills and expertise in special education for working with the parents of these children. Fostering such skills and desirable attitudes in these parents would reduce the sense of futility or the shame parents of mildly impaired children experience, thus reducing the risk of abuse.

We have no criticism of the work of most special educators as they treat parents of children in special education. They do exceedingly well given their tasks and preparation. The problem is that there is often little or no input from special education into general education.

Special education was the first area of education to conduct research and plan programming for abused children. In fact, their work preceded by far most of the efforts by psychologists, physicians, social workers, sociologists, and others. It is too bad that their input is not sought more often.

Parenting Education at Work. In some communities, businesses collaborate on special parenting programs with the schools or community agencies. For example, presenting workshops once per week for several months, in the form of "brown bag" discussions during the workers' lunch hour, can reach large numbers of parents who otherwise are not exposed to important information. In this manner, working parents can learn about effective parenting and about other community resources. Such workshops can be a natural extension of employee assistance programs already operating in many businesses. This is an important area for school-community collaboration.

There is one recent development that may have a beneficial impact if it spreads throughout our business community. We are referring to the development of child care centers and schools at our places of employment. When staffed by trained workers with easy access to parents, not only do the parents and children benefit, but so does business. Ideally, child care centers for teenage parents should be expanded to include any child with a parent at school, whether that parent is a student or an employee.

Other Societal Forces

It is beyond the scope of this book to address those forces external to the school which create conditions which precipitate abuse. There is no doubt but that economic and culture conditions beyond the influence of educators produce stress in the lives of people. Yet this is no reason to believe that education is impotent. By working harder to instill certain values and competencies in students, an important step will be taken to reduce the rate of child maltreatment.

10
TEENAGE PARENTS

Teenage parenthood is a major contributor to the growing problem of child abuse and neglect in the United States and Canada. In the United States the birth rate among adolescents is higher than in any other developed country. About one-quarter of all teenage females become teenage mothers. Even more become pregnant. Each year in the United States, approximately one million teenagers become pregnant, of whom nearly 500,000 give birth.

The overwhelming majority of these pregnancies are unplanned and often unwanted. Nevertheless, approximately 96% of these adolescents keep their offspring. They keep their children regardless of how ill-prepared they are for the responsibilities of parenthood. One result is more abuse and neglect.

From an expense point of view, the financial and human costs of unintended adolescent pregnancies are staggering. Children of teenagers are at a significantly increased risk for a variety of ills. These include low birth weight related health deficiencies and mental and physical impairments. Teenage mothers often receive inadequate prenatal care, are lacking in knowledge about appropriate nutrition, and are at considerable risk of pregnancy complications and poor birth outcomes. In turn, poor birth outcomes further increase the risk of abuse and neglect.

Lack of knowledge and inadequate prenatal care are not the only problems. The majority of teenage parent families are fatherless and living in poverty. Only one-in-five of the fathers will be present at the birth of their children to a teenage mother. Of these, most will be gone from the scene in one year. Even in the cases where the adolescent parents marry, their break-up is extremely likely within a few years. Accompanying this is a disproportionate risk of family violence and the psychological trauma of divorce.

> **Poor self-images, immaturity, financial insecurity, improper bonding, poor social skills, and limited parenting knowledge all create stress. The result is that when young parents face a crisis, they may strike out against their children, or simply ignore and withdraw from them.**

It requires no great leap of the imagination to understand why large numbers of adolescents are not prepared for the rigors of being effective parents. They usually lack maturity, which when combined with stressful contingencies, taxes their ability to cope. Thereby the stage is set for abuse and neglect.

CONTRIBUTING CONDITIONS

Chief among the stressful situations for teenage parents are repeated pregnancies, troubled marriages, social isolation, financial insecurity, having imparied children, and limited parenting knowledge.

Early and Repeated Pregnancies

The environment of the home and neighborhood, peer subcultures, and media influences present even very young children with adult situations and problems which require maturity and judgment to address. A number of social observers note that our youth are "growing up too fast" for the types of pressures and limitations imposed upon them. They claim that childhood as a special time of protection and innocence is disappearing.

> **In essence, many young people are exposed to adult situations wherein they demand or are given the privileges of adulthood, but are incapable of assuming the responsibilities of adults.**

One piece of evidence to support this argument is the high number of young people who are becoming sexually active at a very early age. For example, nearly one-in-five males in the United States has had sexual intercourse *before* the age of fourteen; by the age of twenty, at least 80% of the males and 70% of the females have had intercourse. All too often, early and consistent pressures on teenagers to become sexually active occurs in a context where there is little consideration of contraception. High rates of pregnancy are the result.

Unfortunately, the greatest rate of increase in adolescent pregnancy is among those under age fifteen. Evidence also indicates that approximately six-out-of-ten school-age mothers will have another child while still of school age. Given that their own physical and psychological maturation will still be incomplete, these young parents will be faced with situations requiring mature judgments which they have yet to develop. As has been noted, immaturity is a significant precondition contributing to the abuse and neglect of children.

Single Parenthood

Among the fastest growing family forms are children living with one parent. Teenage mothers are a conspicuous segment of this family type. Among teenage mothers, the overwhelming majority will have out-of-wedlock births. Among those who do marry, the marriage often will be the result of family pressures to avoid the perceived stigma associated with an out-of-wedlock birth. The predictable consequence is a high rate of unhappy marriages among these teenagers. This is reflected in teenage divorce rates which are considerably higher than for any other age group, as well as high levels of domestic violence. If the present trend continues, approximately two-thirds of all children will spend a portion of their lives in a single parent arrangement.

In addition, large numbers of children living with a single parent eventually spend a portion of their childhood or adolescence with a stepparent or a live-in parent surrogate. While it is undoubtedly true that such relationships can be healthy and happy, unfortunately they are often characterized by divided loyalties, conflict and stress. The data reveal a disturbing picture of high rates of physical and sexual abuse in such families. The level of conflict in these families is often cited as contributing to problems such as running away, youth suicide, substance abuse, and a tendency for these youngsters to themselves enter into unhealthy relationships in their adolescence and adulthood.

> **Being a good parent is a difficult task in stable families. Single parenthood greatly complicates the task of raising children, especially if the parent is immature, isolated and lacking financial or other resources.**

Social Isolation

Researchers in countless studies cite *social isolation* as contributing to child abuse and neglect. By social isolation they mean situations where people believe that they cannot rely on others for help. They feel alone even if others are present. How does this feeling of being alone and without help occur among teenage parents?

To illustrate, when an adolescent has a child, very often there is stress between the new mother and her mother. The mother of the teenage parent may not be in a position to help, or she may resent having to assist in her grandchild's care. Conflicts between the young mother and her parents increase feelings of social isolation. The new mother, ill-prepared for the responsibilities of parenthood, finds herself having to rely on the "charity" or good will of her mother or of anyone who will help. But where is the help that reduces stress to be found?

Further contributing to their isolation, approximately 80% of adolescent mothers drop out of school. Not only is their education interrupted or terminated, but they tend to be removed from their network of friends by virtue of even the most minimal of child care that must be provided. If they elect to stay in school, many will find themselves abandoned by their male and female school friends. Even worse, they may continue with the same behavior they exhibited prior to having the child (e.g., drinking, partying to all hours), thus ignoring the needs of their infant. Furthermore, they may be the targets of discriminatory school policies (e.g., not being allowed to participate in extracurricular activities or of receiving honors). It is clear why so many of these adolescents — who crave attention from their peers — feel alone.

Whatever the nature of their isolation, many of these adolescent mothers find themselves taxed to the limit with a feeling that there is no place to turn for help. Under such circumstances, their children are likely to suffer from neglect, or otherwise become scapegoats for parental resentment.

Financial Insecurity

In the United States, somewhere between one-fifth and one-fourth of all children are living in poor families. The majority of these families are headed by single mothers, many of whom are teenagers. Because teenage parents are characterized by chronically low education and unemployment, they stand a strong chance of becoming dependent on some form of public assistance. The cost of welfare for teenage parents and their children is billions and billions of dollars, and the cost continues to rise.

Even with welfare, however, these teenage parents seldom receive enough to provide the health care needed by their children. The lack of a comprehensive program of neonatal care in the country is especially detrimental to the children of these single mothers. This is also true even among teenage parents who are employed because the pay and benefits they receive are too low to maintain basic necessities. For this reason, finding adequate and affordable daycare is a major problem. As a consequence, many are trapped in a chronic state of welfare dependency. Such an existence is fraught with difficulties which contribute to child maltreatment.

Limited Parenting Knowledge

We know from much research that most of the parents who abuse and neglect their children lack even the most rudimentary understanding of their children's basic needs and capabilities. Adolescent parents in particular, by virtue of their lack of experience, often do not grasp their children's physical and emotional requirements. Further complicating that picture, many of these young parents have not been exposed to desirable parent role models. Simply stated, they have not been given the chance to learn to be responsible parents. They have not learned to understand what is needed from them as they seek to meet the needs of their offspring.

> **The inability of many of these parents to provide proper care for their children, in turn, becomes the basis for further eroding their self-esteem.**

Not only are adolescents generally unprepared for parenthood, but they often have difficulty in "bonding" with their offspring. Improper bonding is frequently cited as a condition leading to child abuse and neglect. Problems in bonding — a process critical to the development of healthy parent-child relationships — are especially acute if there are health problems with the infant. Because many teenagers who become pregnant engage in unhealthy practices (e.g., smoking, drinking, drug use, improper dieting) yet do not receive proper prenatal care, it is little surprise that they experience pregnancy complications such as low birth weight babies. Given this condition, medical necessity often forces early separations between teenage parents and their infant children. This too interrupts or retards the bonding process and thereby increases the risk of maltreatment.

Of course, there are healthy and responsible teenage parents who provide nurturing environments for their children. When this happens, seldom have they felt socially isolated. However, it is obvious that the challenges of parenthood are greatly compounded if one is young and lacking healthy models from whom effective parenting skills can be learned. These parents also must cope with social stigma which further exacerbates their difficulties. What then can be done to ameliorate the potential trauma of teenage parenthood?

Fortunately, there are a number of things we can do for teenage parents or parents-to-be that would help to prevent abuse, and we can do them without great cost. We can help both the young fathers and the young mothers in ways which produce fewer school dropouts, higher educational attainments, stronger vocational preparation, and better citizenship. For society, there can be fewer pregnant teenagers, a larger proportion of healthy infants, and improved relationships between these parents and their children.

SCHOOL PROGRAMS

There are compelling health, educational and social reasons why schools should actively attempt to keep pregnant or parenting students in school. Among these is the need to be mindful of our legal obligations.

Legal Considerations

Only a generation ago, it was common for school policies and practices to discourage pregnant and parenting adolescents from regular school attendance. The assumption was that their presence in the classroom was both disruptive to the learning process, and undermined the moral development of other students. Since the 1970's, however, court decisions have reflected the view that pregnancy is not sufficient grounds to deny a student educational opportunity.

In a precedent setting case in 1971 (Ordway *v.* Hargraves), the U.S. District Court found no compelling health reason to warrant the exclusion of a pregnant student from school. It was argued that denial of educational opportunity could cause mental anguish which might negatively impact on the pregnancy. The Court then reasoned that the presence of a pregnant student did not interfere with the school's ability to carry out its functions. The school was ordered to re-admit the student and to allow her to participate in extracurricular activities.

In accord with the changing attitudes of society, our laws now forbid discrimination on the basis of sex. Our laws also protect the rights of pregnant and parenting students. Schools may even be denied funding if they are found to exclude students from educational programs on the basis of pregnancy. In addition, the legal provision of Title IX legislation allow tort action against schools if there is sex discrimination.

> **The conclusion is clear: schools should not arbitrarily dismiss pregnant students. In addition, schools should not assign pregnant students to programs incompatible with the educational and legal rights of other students.**

While our laws suggest what schools should *not* do to pregnant and parenting adolescents, they offer little direction about what schools *should* do in a positive sense. Fortunately, many communities are taking a positive approach. There seems to be an increase in the kinds and number of programs schools are providing to students during pregnancy and parenthood. This is a hopeful trend in terms of child abuse prevention. While there is considerable variation in how this assistance is provided, the most common approach is to offer some form of parenting education.

Parenting Education for New Parents

In the previous chapter, we suggested that parenting education should be integrated throughout the curriculum and available to all students. This comprehensive approach also includes special programming for pregnant and parenting students.

In the broadest sense, this special programming involves targeting new parents and parents-to-be for the purpose of enhancing their parental competencies. It recognizes that effective parenting is an acquired skill which can be enhanced among students if there are appropriate curriculum experiences.

Of course parenting education varies in emphasis, quality and comprehensiveness. At present, most schools give some attention to those students who are pregnant, perhaps through family living or other courses. Some also provide for those who are in programs which are similar to those which used to be called "programs for unwed mothers," a most unfortunate characterization, indeed. More recently, the movement has been to provide parenting information to teenage parents along with child care services. A few schools also offer programs for the *parents* of pregnant or teenage parents. These grandparents — usually the grandmother — often assume a major role in childrearing. Regardless of the programs offered, however, the quality programs seek to:

- provide needed prenatal and postnatal care information;

- motivate young parents to make mature, responsible and informed decisions;

- assist them in resolving their personal, family, vocational and academic problems which are related to their pregnancy or parenthood;

- increase the probabilities that they will complete their secondary education;

- provide guidance which decreases the likelihood of repeated pregnancies;

- identify those at high risk of being abusive or neglectful parents and assist them in obtaining help; and

- provide instruction which helps them become more well-adjusted, nurturing, competent and non-abusing persons.

Helping Young Fathers

Teenage males often are overlooked in adolescent pregnancy or parenting programs. Yet teenage fathers usually play a critical role in the mother's decision to engage in sexual activity, to use contraceptives, whether to stay in school, and whether to be a positive force in the lives of her children. It is therefore important to understand the special circumstances surrounding teenage fathers, and to offer them a helpful education.

Teenage fathers, however, are by no means a homogeneous group. They display considerable variation in their backgrounds, in their level of maturity, and in their willingness to be active in raising their offspring. The common stereotype is of a lower class minority male, who preys upon and impregnates females, whose manhood is equated with sexual prowess, and who ultimately abdicates all responsibility for both mother and child. While it is true that minorities are over-represented in the statistics on teenage pregnancy, such stereotypes are unfortunate and do not portray the complete picture.

What do we know about teenage fathers? Research on adolescent fathers suggests several common features:

- Teenage fathers often become sexually active at an early age (around fourteen). Their sexual intercourse tends to be with someone with whom they were "going steady." This suggests an emotional commitment to their partners, rather than being simply "Don Juans." Unfortunately, this emotional involvement takes place in the context of limited knowledge of human sexuality and birth control, and limited experience in committed relationships. There also is likely to be a fundamental immaturity in terms of assuming responsibility for the consequences of their actions.

- Adolescent fathers-to-be often experience difficulty in coping with a pregnancy for which they are responsible. Like their female mates, they exhibit considerable confusion over their impending parenthood, ranging from deep anxiety to a highly unrealistic and romanticized view of the parent role. This suggests that they are not totally uncaring about their status as future parents. Rather, fathers-to-be, without assistance, usually lack the knowledge, skills and values to be good parents. In this regard they are like young mothers-to-be.

- Many adolescent fathers express a willingness to provide financial support and a desire to help care for their offspring. Often, however, they are denied the opportunity to help. In some cases the mother moves away or the parents of the adolescent mother denies the father access to the child. Depending upon the situation, excluding a teenage father from assuming an active role in parenting may contribute to child abuse or neglect by the mother. Whatever the case, teenage fathers need to be carefully considered for what they might positively contribute.

With these observations in mind, schools should strive to do all they can to emphasize the importance of responsible fatherhood in the context of parent education programs. This means that schools should seek to aggressively involve teenage fathers in parent programming, and attempt to break down the social pressures and stigma which discourage their involvement as responsible parents.

> **Failure to actively involve teenage fathers in parent programs may perpetuate a self-fulfilling prophecy in which males create more problems for their children and mates. These problems can include acts of commission (e.g., violence), as well as omission (e.g., disengaging from being a parent).**

It is ironic, indeed, that we lament the large numbers of single teenage mothers, while unintentionally ignoring or discouraging young males from being responsible in their relationships. What is even more disheartening is that many irresponsible teenage fathers carry on to become irresponsible adult fathers. Thus, programming for males should strive to do the following:

- encourage responsible decision making regarding sexual activity, while teaching about the nature and meaning of commitment between couples;

- promote responsible involvement in the parenting process whenever appropriate;

- foster skills and competence in the area of child care;

- decrease the likelihood of dropping out of school; and

- enhance desirable vocational and educational decision making which increases the prospects of socioeconomic independence.

The Need for Support Services

Perhaps the most critical support service a school can offer teenage parents is to provide help with child care while they are in school. Through such service they can provide "hands on" guidance in parenting which diminishes the probabilities of abuse or neglect. This means giving special attention to health care, counseling and referral services.

Health Care. Health care services are an important component of an effective teenage parenting program. Included here are health and nutrition counseling. In addition, some school systems, in cooperation with local health organizations, have weekly prenatal and infant clinics offered in the school buildings. These clinics allow for regular health assessments of children and their parents. Some schools also collaborate with health organizations in arranging home visits for new born infants. Our view is that a systematic program of neonatal home visitation would significantly reduce rates of child maltreatment. Even where regular neonatal home visits are not possible, many schools have their own home-bound programs where teachers work with the teenagers at home until they can attend school.

Counseling Services. Counseling is another critical element in a successful teenage parenting program. The need for vocational counseling is especially important due to the economic necessities faced by school-aged mothers and fathers. Along with such counseling, there needs to be employment training. These classes should teach students how to find and keep a job if they choose not to attend college. Assistance should also be given to help them locate appropriate employment which does not interfere with their schooling or parenting.

> **Given the very high rates of child maltreatment in homes characterized by chronic unemployment, job skills training and job placement services constitute important elements in abuse prevention programming.**

Referral Services. One of the most important support services schools can provide is to be a referral agent. This involves identifying needs among students and making timely referrals to the appropriate school or community service agencies. It also involves teaching students about available supports within the community and school, and helping them evaluate these sources of support. In the long run, fostering the ability to make self-referral among teenage parents results in greater numbers of potentially abusive parents finding help before a crisis develops.

Parents of Teenage Parents. It is obvious that the effectiveness of a program for teenage parents will hinge on its capacity to take into account their particular circumstances, both in and outside of school. One of the most important considerations in their lives is their own parents. Since the parents of teenage mothers and fathers are usually influential, it is important that procedures be in place to work with them. Adolescent mothers are especially likely to seek the counsel of their mothers regarding child rearing. Furthermore, the mother of a teenage parent may be the primary caregiver for both her grandchild and daughter as her daughter goes about the business of being an adolescent. Many excellent school-based child care programs go out of their way to involve all those who are involved as care givers.

Providing health care, counseling, referral and family services to teenage parents and parents-to-be constitutes the one area of major added expense in a basic prevention program. However, there is increasing recognition of the need for government sponsored school-based programs. It is therefore important to encourage federal, regional and local governmental units to lend their support because it will cost them more if they ignore teenage parents. Fortunately, there is some evidence that government is slowly responding. Most schools are finding that some private funding is also available. While this is encouraging, we have a long way to go in helping teenage parents if we want to produce a less criminal and deficient social order.

11
UNDERSTANDING
COMMUNITY RESISTANCE

Not everyone agrees that schools should be in the business of solving social problems, especially those involving the family. Some argue that the role of our schools should be limited to teaching the basics such as reading, writing, mathematics and other traditional academic subjects. Some argue that our schools lack the expertise and the resources necessary to address the complexities of child development, particularly as impacted by abuse. Some assert that the task of reducing child abuse and neglect is best left to law enforcement and to social work professionals outside the school.

We agree that our schools should be in the business of teaching academic skills. We disagree, however, that there are no other goals for education or that abuse is irrelevant to academic learning. Most people recognize that being abused is an impairment to effective school learning, just as is a physical or mental impairment, two conditions which society demands that educators take into account in their curricula.

We also disagree that our schools lack the expertise or resources to help our students become good citizens, including learning to be good parents. We also disagree with those who believe the schools have no right to seek to reduce pregnancies among young people. Yet because there is opposition, there seems to be a tendency for some schools to do the minimum in order to satisfy both sides.

If the development of good citizenship as the foundation of primary prevention is to be successful, then serious and long-term commitments by our schools and communities are essential. Token efforts will be insufficient. Thankfully, the basic approach we have suggested will not consume excessive time or resources; nor will it interfere with an emphasis on teaching knowledge and critical thinking skills. In fact, an effective primary prevention effort can be included in the cost of current school expenditures.

Even so, there will continue to be opposition. Are the concerns of those opposed to primary prevention of abuse justified?

Much of the opposition focuses on sexual abuse prevention. On the surface, it appears that at least some of the criticism of sexual abuse prevention is *politically* motivated. Some oppose these programs on the grounds that they are deceptive attempts at introducing "sex education" and are therefore taking away the rights of parents. Admittedly, the issue of sex education is complex and fraught with controversy.

From our point of view, however, efforts to castigate programs that emphasize knowledge and competencies for responsible behavior on the grounds of simply being pernicious attempts at sex education are ill-informed. In fact, when the community is made aware that teaching respect and responsibility is the central focus, then much of this opposition should subside.

There are other concerns regarding sexual abuse prevention that are worthy of consideration. For example, consider the cautiousness of some people over teaching young children about "good touches" and "bad touches." Certainly it is necessary and desirable to teach children how to recognize and to refuse inappropriate touching. However, there is a danger that if these ideas are not taught correctly, then young children may overreact to include "good touches" among "bad touches."

> **While it is desirable to provide children with the vocabulary to identify feelings related to touch, great care should be taken so that they do not misinterpret appropriate parental behavior.**

Some critics also fear that teaching about "bad touches" will lead children to make false reports of sexual abuse (though there is little evidence that this has occurred). It is also feared by some that young children will unintentionally learn to reject appropriate medical care. There is no hard data to support this conclusion either. Yet caution is clearly warranted in order to be sure that hyperbole and exaggeration is avoided in teaching about "bad touches." Furthermore, in regard to teaching children about legitimate and illegitimate touches, the child's level of development is important. This should be made clear to the parents who are concerned about what is taught.

Another source of opposition to information being presented on abuse is a concern for adolescents experimenting with sexual behavior. Teenagers are likely to experience a great deal of ambiguity and confusion about touching. Teaching in simplistic ways about "bad touch" may not adequately address this confusion.

Furthermore, most teenagers will not go to adults for help in clarifying all the puzzling aspects of a sexual situation. Thus, programming for teenagers should carefully address the complexity of adolescent relationships and should provide them with realistic ways of dealing with their feelings.

Teaching children to resist being victimized is also a concern for some people. Without question, the ability to resist is desirable. Few argue about this. However, in teaching children how to react effectively to an abuse situation, we must be careful not to impose on them the felt responsibility for their self-protection. We know that "self-defense" in terms of active physical resistance is highly improbable with very young children. In addition, given their state of physical and moral development, asserting that young children can always say "no" to adult authority is not realistic; the power imbalance is simply too great.

In the approach we suggest, self-protection is best defined as fostering the knowledge and skills to identify an abuse situation and to seek appropriate help. Effective prevention addresses these concerns for protecting self by promoting trust in balance with caution. Effective programs are careful in making sure that children do not develop a generalized fear or distrust of all adults, including males. Children need to feel security and trust in the care of adults, especially their family members, when it is so warranted.

Model prevention programs make possible the identification of abuse while simultaneously placing heavy emphasis on the idea that most adults do not harm children.

We believe that most educators, as well as large portions of society, will support a basic integrated prevention program which stresses teaching about rights and responsibilities. The danger, however, is that school boards may settle for a "quick fix" approach to prevention, such as bringing in an occasional guest speaker or showing a film on sexual abuse. This does little to empower children with the knowledge, skills or attitudes to avoid abuse or to seek help. Quick fixes also do little to prepare and foster in educators an acceptance of their responsibilities. To the contrary, such easy "solutions" are likely to be counterproductive in that they create the *illusion* that the problem is being addressed, when in fact it is not.

Whatever the potential caveats, however, it is clear that the problem of abused children is enormous and the need for integrated basic abuse prevention programs — in other words, programming for healthy parenting — in our schools is great.

We agree with the conclusion offered by the U.S.
Advisory Board on Child Abuse and Neglect (1990): U.S.
taxpayers spend ". . . billions of dollars on programs that
deal with the results of the nation's failure to prevent . . .
child abuse and neglect." The Board urges educators,
politicians, and citizens to ". . . view the prevention of
child abuse and neglect as a matter of national security."

12
EPILOGUE

Evidence is accumulating that societal conditions which give rise to child maltreatment are getting worse. We believe that there is an increase in child abuse and neglect which cannot be explained away by an increase in reporting. Simply stated, the problem is going from bad to worse because of changes in the way people live.

Changes in the family illustrate the problem. As previously discussed, there is an increasing number of children living with multiple stepparents without benefit of proper bonding. There is an overwhelming increase in the number of teenage parents who are ill-equipped to raise their offspring. Alcoholism and other substance abuse are on the rise. More and more, both parents are required to be employed in order to survive above the poverty level. Added to this are the many changes in prerequisites to gain employment, and the related work requirements that conflict with parents' needs to be with their children.

The decline of our cities, coupled with the rise of juvenile gang and other violence, means that many of our young grow up not only impoverished, but surrounded by the constant threat of unsafe streets. They are literally prisoners within urban war zones. Even if their homes are relatively stable — and many are not — these children are victimized by the violence in their community. They feel unsafe because they are unsafe. A predator-prey mentality dominates the daily ethic of these young people. This in turn encourages them to join gangs or seek other unhealthy peer attachments which offer them a felt sense of safety and belonging. Gang life, however, only further isolates them from access to legitimate avenues of success and support in society. Unstable communities thus contribute directly to unstable families.

In addition, children and adolescents are being increasingly isolated from their grandparents, cousins, aunts and uncles, and even from their siblings by the character of how entertainment is provided. When families are together, they spend half of that time watching television. They are physically together but psychologically isolated. This isolation makes it difficult for healthy family interactions and support to occur. Each child seemingly goes his or her own way, becoming almost a stranger to other family members.

Poverty, unemployment, insufficient health care programs, inadequate day care, and stresses in the workplace directly contribute to the malfunctioning of families. The list goes on and on, but the point is clear: family life today is fraught with problems which place children at risk. The end result is that masses of our young find less and less gratification in family life. As they reach adolescence, many look for compensation in the analgesics of alcohol or illicit drugs, in sexual activity, in unhealthy entertainments, and in criminal gangs or other unhealthy attachments to peers.

Some social critics believe our society is increasingly narcissistic and self-absorbed. In the end, such narcissism sets the stage for the exploitation of others. Whatever the merits of this view, one conclusion is obvious: abuse, neglect and exploitation become the basis for future abuse, neglect and exploitation. The pattern mirrors itself in that many victims become victimizers.

We believe that healthy families are the bedrock of a healthy society. When a large proportion of people suffer in their family lives, democracy is threatened. Democracy requires an intellectually, economically, and psychologically healthy body of citizens. The many serious outcomes which can result from abuse or neglect — delinquency, drug dependencies, running away, dropping out, suicide, violence and continued exploitation of others, to mention a few — rend asunder the very fabric of society.

To impair the competencies of citizens through abuse is to harm society itself.

Large numbers of dysfunctional families produce large scale personal disorganization, a decline of law and order, and a breakdown of social cohesion — what philosophers refer to as the social contract. Social cohesion around a compatible set of democratic values is critical for the maintenance of a healthy democracy. Thus, how parents treat our young is of cardinal importance for the kind of society we desire.

With consequences for democracy in mind, we again return to the vexing question of how to halt child abuse and neglect. Clearly we cannot send trained professionals into every home to observe children and to teach good parenting. Such a "big brother" approach would violate the personal rights and values we hold dear. Furthermore, it would be too late to wait until people reach adulthood to teach them how to be decent to one another. By then, the damage is done and the task is overwhelming, even for trained therapists.

Our alternative is to use the public schools to teach all young people how to be good parents. In a democracy, the public schools belong to the public; and the public has a right to expect schools to promote the core skills, knowledge, and values necessary to sustain society. The school is the only organization which is subject in considerable detail to public policy and which can teach people respect for human dignity.

Teaching the competencies associated with effective parenting and healthy family life is as important as the traditional basic skills of reading, writing and arithmetic. Curricular experiences in healthy human relations should be required of all students, starting very early and continuing throughout secondary school.

One goal remains: to help those who are abused. The desirable long-term goal, however, is to teach all how not to be abusive. As citizens, our activities differ but several of our objectives for young people should be the same. We need to help all young people:

- reduce inappropriate feelings of helplessness;

- increase relationships with nonexploitive people;

- manage feelings of guilt, anger and mistrust;

- learn what characterizes abuse, neglect and exploitation;

- acquire the skills and motivation to extricate themselves from exploitive relationships;

- develop their abilities to deal with abusive people when it is not possible to break off a relationship with them;

- find avenues of support where they can talk about what has happened to them without fear of reprisal or stigma;

- learn to value and to create nonexploitive relationships with their mates, children, parents and peers; and

- in summary, learn that respect for human dignity is a critical part of being a decent citizen in a democratic society.

Since our fundamental concern is for the total society of individuals, the burden of helping to end child abuse must be shouldered by all of us. To do this we must encourage our schools to lead the way. The cycles of violence and human misery can be broken when we are effective in teaching parents and parents-to-be that they need not abuse, neglect or exploit others. This is an immense challenge, but with the help of our schools, it is a challenge we are capable of meeting.

It is true that we do not have all the answers to the question of child abuse prevention. It is also true that current efforts to reduce child abuse are extremely limited in focus and energy. However, our schools are expanding their scope to empower children both to resist abuse and to become non-abusive parents. We believe that these developments represent a healthy sign.

There is another hopeful sign. In recent years there has been a proliferation of educational materials for reducing child abuse. These materials are being integrated into the regular curriculum without slighting other educational objectives. Perhaps one day nearly all educators will incorporate prevention of abuse into their classrooms without negatively affecting their other academic and social tasks.

Even though we have an incomplete understanding of how to eliminate child abuse, we now know enough to institute important prevention efforts. As educators, we are compelled to make this effort. Our children are our future. They have a right to a life free of the trauma of abuse or neglect because we all have a right to a more sane and humane society.

Appendix A
Format for a Child Abuse and Neglect Policy*

Components	Components to be Cited	Sample Wording
1. Rationale for Policy	A brief rationale for involving school personnel in reporting.	Because of their sustained contact with school-age children, school employees are in an excellent position to identify abused or neglected children and to refer them for treatment and protection.
	The name and appropriate section numbers of the state reporting statue.	To comply with the Mandatory Reporting of Child Abuse and Neglect Act (Sections 3851-3860 Maine Revised Statues (1975 found in Title 22, Chapter 1056).
2. Legal Obligations	Reportable conditions as defined by state law.	...who know or has reasonable cause to suspect that a child has been subjected to abuse or neglect or observes the child being subjected to conditions or circumstances which would reasonably result in abuse...
	The exact language of the law to define "abuse" and "neglect," if necessary, explain clarify or expand.	"Child abuse and neglect" means physical and mental injury, sexual abuse, negligent treatment or maltreatment of a child under the age of 18 years by a person who is responsible for the child's welfare under circumstances which indicate that the child's health or welfare is harmed or threatened thereby.

*Adapted from Child Abuse and Neglect Project, Education Commission of the States. Report No. 85 Education Policies and Practices Regarding Child Abuse and Neglect and Recommendations for Policy Development (April 1976).

	Components	Components to be Cited	Sample Working
2.	Legal Obligations (continued)	Whether or not there is immunity from civil liability and criminal penalty for those who report or participate in an investigation or judicial proceeding; and whether immunity is for good faith reporting.	In Maine, anyone making a report in accordance with the state law or participating in a resulting judicial proceeding is presumed to be acting in good faith and, in doing so, is immune from any civil or criminal liability that might otherwise be imposed.
		Penalty for failure to report.	Failure to report may result in a misdemeanor charge: punishment by a fine up to $500.
3.	Professional Obligations	Any provision of the law regarding the confidentiality of records pertaining to reports of suspected abuse or neglect.	All records concerning reports of suspected abuse or neglect are confidential. Anyone who permits, assists or encourages the release of information from records to a person or agency not legally permitted to have access may be guilty of a misdemeanor.
		Who specifically is mandated to report and (if applicable) who may report.	...it is the policy of the _____ School District that any teacher or other school employee...
		The person or agency to receive reports.	...shall report to the building principal or his or her designated agent who shall then be responsible for making the report to the Department of Human Services...

Appendix B
A Flow Chart of Protective Services*

REPORT FROM SCHOOL
Building Child Abuse and Neglect (CAN) team reports the possibility of child maltreatment to the appropriate community agency.

↓

INVESTIGATION
Appropriate community agency (e.g., Department of Human Services, Family and Children's Services, etc.) receives report and investigates case.

↓

EVALUATION
Legal, educational, medical and mental health aspects of case are evaluated; a determination of abuse or neglect is made and the possibility of further risk is evaluated.

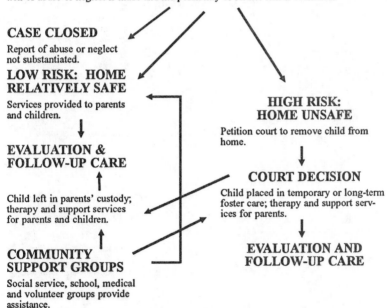

CASE CLOSED
Report of abuse or neglect not substantiated.

LOW RISK: HOME RELATIVELY SAFE
Services provided to parents and children.

HIGH RISK: HOME UNSAFE
Petition court to remove child from home.

EVALUATION & FOLLOW-UP CARE

Child left in parents' custody; therapy and support services for parents and children.

COURT DECISION
Child placed in temporary or long-term foster care; therapy and support services for parents.

COMMUNITY SUPPORT GROUPS
Social service, school, medical and volunteer groups provide assistance.

EVALUATION AND FOLLOW-UP CARE

*A flow chart similar to the one above should be developed for each district and provided to all school staff.

Appendix C
Sample Child Abuse Report Form

Name of child: _____

Age: _____   Sex: _____

Address: _____

_____

Grade: _____

Parent(s) or Guardian(s):

_____

Address: _____

_____

Home Phone: _____   Work Phone: _____

Date: _____

Composition of Family:

_____

Type of suspected abuse or neglect:

❑ Fracture   ❑ Beating   ❑ Burns

❑ Cuts/Bruises/Welts ❑ Shaking   ❑ Abandonment

❑ Physical neglect   ❑ Medical neglect

❑ Lack of supervision ❑ Emotional abuse

❑ Sexual abuse   ❑ Malnutrition

Remarks:

_____

_____

Time, place and conditions prompting report:

_____

_____

_____

Child's account of injury or situation:

_____

_____

_____

_____

Known previous instances of maltreatment involving child or siblings:

_____

_____

Person(s) responsible for suspected abuse or neglect:

_____

_____

Person(s) known to witness incident:

_____

_____

Actions taken to assist child (if any):

_____

_____

Person/agency receiving report:

_____

_____

Comments:

_____

_____

_____

Name of person reporting:

_____

Position: _____

Phone: _____

Signature: _____

Date report submitted: _____

Appendix D
Sample Child Abuse Follow-up Form

Child's name: _____

Age: _____   Sex: _____

Child's address: _____

_____

Grade: _____

Parent(s) or guardian(s) name:

_____

Conditions prompting initial report:

_____

_____

_____

_____

_____

Current Behavioral Assessments of Child

School Attendance:

_____

Academic Performance:

_____

Peer Relationships:

_____

Relationships with teachers:

_____

Relationship with non-abusive parent:

_____

_____

_____

Relationship with abuser:

_____

_____

_____

Behavioral or emotional problems encountered:

_____

_____

_____

_____

Actions taken by school on behalf of child:

_____

_____

_____

_____

_____

Information obtained from protective services or other sources:

_____

_____

_____

_____

Interventions taken by protective services or others:

_____

_____

_____

_____

_____

Suggested school interventions for child

_____

_____

_____

_____

_____

Comments:

_____

_____

_____

_____

_____

Name of Person Recording:

_____

Position: _____

Phone: _____

Signature: _____

Date Submitted: _____

Appendix E
Resource Organizations in the
United States and Canada

AA World Services
P. O. Box 475, Riverside Drive
New York, NY 10163
(212) 870-3400

Al-Anon Family Group Headquarters
P. O. Box 862, Midtown Station
New York, NY 10018
(212) 302-7240

Alateen Family Group Headquarters
Box 182, Madison Square Garden
New York, NY 10159-0182
(212) 683-1771

Alcohol & Drug Problem Association of North America
444 N. Capitol Street, NW, Ste 706
Washington, DC 20001
(202) 737-4340

American Academy of Pediatrics
141 Northwest Point Blvd.
P. O. Box 927
Elk Grove Village, IL 60009-0927
708-228-5005

American Association for Counseling & Development
5999 Stevenson Avenue
Alexandria, VA 22304
(703) 823-9800

American Association for Marriage and Family Therapy
1100 17th Street, NW
Washington, DC 20036
(202) 452-0109

American Association of Pastoral Counselors
4505A Lee Highway
Fairfax, VA 22031-2303
(703) 385-6967

American Bar Association
National Legal Resource Center for
Child Advocacy and Protection
1800 M Street, NW, Suite 200
Washington, DC 20036
(202) 331-2250

American Council for Drug Education
204 Monroe Street, Ste 110
Rockville, MD 20850
(301) 294-0600

American Humane Association
Children's Division
63 Iverness Drive E.
Englewood, CO 80112-5117

American Medical Association
Health and Human Behavior Department
515 N. State Street
Chicago, IL 60610
(312) 464-4818

**American Professional Society
On the Abuse of Children**
332 South Michigan Avenue, Ste 1600
Chicago, IL   60604

American Public Health Association
1015 15th Street, NW
Washington, DC 20005
(202) 789-5600

American Public Welfare Association
810 1st Street N.E., Ste 500
Washington, DC 20002-4267

Batterers Anonymous
8485 Tamarind, Ste D
Fortuna, CA 92335
(714) 335-1100

Boys and Girls Clubs of America
771 1st Avenue
New York, NY 10017
(212) 351-5900

Canadian Criminal Justice Association
55 Parkdale Ave.
Ottawa, Ontario K1Y 1E5
(613) 725-3715

Carnegie Council on Adolescent Development
c/o Carnegie Corporation
437 Madison Avenue
New York, NY 10022
(212) 371-3200

Center for Child Protection and Family Support
714 G Street, SE
Washington, DC 20003

Childhelp USA
6463 Independence Avenue
Woodland Hills, CA 91370
1-800-4-A-CHILD

Child Find America
P.O. Box 277
New Platz, NY 12561
(914) 255-1848

Child Welfare Institute
1365 Peachtree Street, NE, Ste 700
Atlanta, GA 30309

Child Welfare League of America
440 1st Street NW, Ste 310
Washington, DC 20001

Children of Alcoholics Foundation
P.O. Box 4185, Grand Central Station
New York, NY 10163-4185
(212) 754-0656

Children's Defense Fund
25 East St., NW
Washington, DC 20001
(202) 628-8787

Covenant House
346 W. 17th Street
New York, NY 10011-5002
(212) 727-4000

The Family Resource Coalition
2001 S. Michigan Avenue, Ste 1520
Chicago, IL 60604
(312) 341-0900

Family Violence and Sexual Assault Institute
1310 Clinic Drive
Tyler, TX 75702

Hazelden Foundation
15245 Pleasant Valley Road, P.O. Box 11
Center City, MN 55012-0011
(612) 257-4010

National Assault Prevention Center
P. O. Box 02005
Columbus, OH 43202
(614) 291-2540

National Association for Children of Alcoholics
11426 Rockville Pike, Ste 100
Rockville, MD 20852
(301) 468-0985

National Association of Public Child Welfare
Administrators (NAPCWA)
810 1st Street N.E., Ste 500
Washington, DC 20002-4267
(202) 682-0100

National Association of Secondary School Principals
1904 Association Drive
Reston, VA 22091
(703) 860-0200

National Association of Social Workers
750 1st Street, N.E., Ste 700
Silver Spring, MD 20910
(202) 408-8600

National Black Child Development Institute
1023 15th Street, N.E., Ste 600
Washington, DC 20005
(202) 387-1281

National Center for Missing and Exploited Children
Education, Prevention, and Public Awareness Division
2101 Wilson Blvd., Ste 550
Arlington, VA 22201-3052
(703) 235-3900

National Center on Child Abuse and Neglect
P. O. Box 1182
Washington, DC 20013
(703) 385-7565

National Center on Child Abuse Prevention Research
332 S. Michigan Avenue, Suite 950
Chicago, IL 60604
(312) 663-3520

National Child Safety Council
P. O. Box 1368
4065 Page Avenue
Jackson, MI 49204
(517) 764-6070

National Clearinghouse for Alcohol and Drug Information
P.O. Box 2345
Rockville, MD 20847-2345

National Clearinghouse on Child Abuse and Neglect
3998 Fair Ridge Drive, Ste 350
Fairfax, VA 22033

National Clearinghouse on Family Violence
Health Canada
#1108, Finance Building
Tunney's Pasture
Ottawa, CANADA   K1A 1B5

National Clearinghouse on Runaway and Homeless Youth
P.O. Box 13505
Silver Spring, MD   20911-3505

National Coalition Against Domestic Violence
P.O. Box 34103
Washington, DC   20043-4103
(202) 638-6388

National Coalition Against Sexual Assault (NCASA)
P.O. Box 21378
Washington, DC   20009
(202) 483-7165

National Committee for Prevention of Child Abuse (NCPCA)
332 S. Michigan, Suite 1600
Chicago, IL   60604-4357
(617) 423-4620

National Conference of State Legislatures
1560 Broadway, Ste 700
Denver, CO   80202
(303) 830-2200

National Council of Juvenile and Family Court Judges
P. O. Box 8970
Reno, NV   89507
(702) 784-6012

National Council on Alcoholism and Drug Dependence
12 W. 21st Street
New York, NY   10010
(212) 206-6770

National Council on Child Abuse and Family Violence
1155 Connecticut Avenue, NW, Suite 300
Washington, DC 20036
1-800-222-2000

National Crime Prevention Council
1700 K Street, NW
Washington, DC 20006-3817
(202) 466-6272

National Education Association
1201 16th Street NW
Washington, DC 20036
(202) 833-4000

National Federation of Parents for Drug-Free Youth
11159 B South Town Sq.
St. Louis, MO 63123
(314) 845-1933

National Information Clearinghouse
For Infants with Disabilities
Center for Developmental Disabilities
USC/Benson Building
Columbia, SC 29208

National Institute of Alcoholism and Alcohol Abuse
5600 Fishers Lane
Rockville, MD 20857

National Network of Children's Advocacy Centers
301 Randolph Avenue
Huntsville, AL 35801

The National Network of Runaway and Youth Services
1319 F Street, NW, Ste 401
Washington, DC 20004
(800) 621-4000

National Organization on Adolescent
Pregnancy and Parenting
4421A East-West Highway
Bethesda, MD 20814
(301) 913-0378

National Organization for Victim Assistance (NOVA)
1757 Park Road, NW
Washington, DC 20010
(202) 232-6682

National Parents' Resource Institute for Drug Education
50 Aurt Plaza, Ste 210
Atlanta, GA 30303
(404) 577-4500

National Prevention Network
444 N. Capitol Street, NW, #642
Washington, DC 20001
(202) 783-6868

National Resource Center on Child Abuse and Neglect
63 Iverness Drive East
Englewood, CO   80112-5117

National Resource Center on Child Sexual Abuse
107 Lincoln Street
Huntsville, AL   35801

The National Runaway Switchboard
Metro-Help, Inc.
3050 N. Lincoln Avenue
Chicago, IL 60657
(800) 621-4000

National School Boards Association
1680 Duke Street
Alexandria, VA 22314
(703) 838-6722

National Victims Resource Center
Office for Victims of Crime
633 Indiana Avenue, NW
Washington, DC   20531

Office of Juvenile Justice and Delinquency Prevention
1600 Research Blvd., 2B
Rockville, MD   20850

Parents Anonymous
520 S. Lafayette Park Place, Ste 316
Los Angeles 90057
(213) 388-6685

Planned Parenthood Federation of America
Department of Education
810 Seventh Avenue
New York, NY 10019
(212) 541-7800

**Sex Information and Education Council
of the United States**
130 W 42nd Street, Ste 2500
New York, NY 10036
(212) 819-9770

YMCA of the United States
101 N. Wacker Drive
Chicago, IL 60606
(312) 977-0031

YWCA of the United States
726 Broadway
New York, NY 10003
(212) 614-2700

228 *ABUSED CHILDREN*

SELECTED BIBLIOGRAPHY

231 R. *Children of Alcoholics* (2nd ed.). Holmes Beach, FL: Learning Publications, Inc., 1983.

Ackerman, D.M. and Cohen, H. *The constitutionality of excessive corporal punishment in schools.* Washington, D.C.: Congressional Research Service Report #88-143A, 1988.

American Association for Protecting Children. *Highlights of Official Child Neglect and Abuse Reporting: 1986.* Washington, D.C.: American Humane Association, 1989.

Bartlette, D. "Child abuse and developmental disabilities." *Virginia Child Protection Newsletter,* Vol. 37, Fall 1992.

Besharov, D. *Recognizing Child Abuse.* New York:Free Press, 1990.

Besharov, D.J. *Contending with overblown expectations.* Public Welfare 45(1): 7-11, 1987.

Besharov, D.J. The legal framework for child protection. pp. 149-154 in C.M. Mouzakitis and R. Varghese (eds.). *Social Work Treatment With Abused and Neglected Children.* Springfield, IL: Charles C. Thomas, 1985.

Blumenkrantz, David. *Fulfilling the Promise of Children's Services.* San Francisco: Josey-Bass Publishers, 1992.

Broadhurst, D.D. *The Role of Law Enforcement in the Prevention and Treatment of Child Abuse and Neglect.* Washington: U.S. Department of Health and Human Services, 1984.

Bross, D.B. "The legal basis for child protection teams." in D.B. Bross et.al. (eds.). *The New Child Protection Team Handbook.* New York: Garland, 1988.

Cassell, C. and Wilson, P. *Sexuality Education: A Resource Book.* New York: Aldyne De Gruyter, 1989.

Cherlin, A. *The Changing American Family and Public Policy.* Washington, D.C.: The Urban Institute Press, 1988.

Children's Defense Fund. *Adolescent Pregnancy: Whose Problem Is It?* Washington, D.C.: Adolescent Pregnancy Prevention Clearinghouse, 1986.

Children's Defense Fund. *Model Programs: Preventing Adolescent Pregnancy and Building Youth Self-Sufficiency.* Washington, D.C.: Adolescent Pregnancy Prevention Clearinghouse, 1986.

Children's Defense Fund. *Preventing Children Having Children.* Washington, D.C.: Adolescent Pregnancy Prevention Clearinghouse, 1985.

Chilman, C.C., Cox, F., and E. Nunnally (eds.). *Families in Trouble.* Newbury Park, CA: Sage Publications, 1988.

Colorado Department of Education. *The School's Role in the Prevention/Intervention of Child Abuse and Neglect: A Handbook for School Personnel.* Denver: Colorado Department of Education, 1988.

Crow, G. and Crow, L. *Crisis Intervention and Suicide Prevention: Working with Children and Adolescents.* Springfield, IL: Charles C. Thomas, 1987.

Daro, D., Casey, K. and N. Abrahams. *Reducing Child Abuse 20% by 1990: Preliminary Assessment.* Chicago, IL: National Committee for Prevention of Child Abuse, 1990.

Daro, D. *Confronting Child Abuse: Research for Effective Program Design.* New York: The Free Press, 1988.

Dattalo, P. "The Gentrification of Public Welfare." *Social Work,* 37, 446-453, 1992.

Davis, S.M. and Schwartz, M.D. *Children's Rights and the Law.* Lexington, MA: Lexington Books, 1987.

Department of Health and Human Services, *Study of National Incidence of Child Abuse and Neglect.* Washington, D.C.: Contract 105-85-1702, 1988.

Ebeling, N. and Hill, D., (eds.). *Child Abuse and Neglect.* Littleton, MA: PSG Publishing, 1983.

Education Commission of the States. *Education Policies and Practices Regarding Child Abuse and Neglect and Recommendations for Policy Development.* Child Abuse Project, Denver, Colorado, Report No. 85, April, 1976.

Elster, A.B. and Lamb, M.E. (eds.). *Adolescent Fatherhood.* Hillsdale, NJ: Lawrence Erlbaum, 1986.

Faller, K. (ed). *Social Work with Abused and Neglected Children.* New York: Free Press, 1981.

Finklehor, David. *Stopping Family Violence: Research Priorities for the Coming Decade.* Newbury Park, CA: Sage Publications, Inc., 1988.

Finklehor, David. "The Trauma of Child Sexual Abuse." *Journal of Interpersonal Violence,* Vol. 2, No. 4, December 1987.

Finklehor, David. *Child Sexual Abuse.* New York: Free Press, 1984.

Finklehor, David. *Sexually Victimized Children.* New York: Free Press, 1979.

Garbarino, J., Dubrow, N. Kostelny, K., and C. Pardo. *Children in Danger: Coping with the Consequences of Community Violence.* San Francisco, CA: Josey Bass, 1992.

Garbarino, J. and K. Kostelny. "Child Maltreatment as a Community Problem." *Child Abuse and Neglect,* 1992.

Garbarino, J., Kostelny, K., and N. Dubrow. *No Place to Be a Child: Growing Up in a War Zone.* Lexington, MA: Lexington Books, 1991.

Garbarino, J., Brookhouser, P. Authier, K. and associates. *Special Children — Special Risks: The Maltreatment of Children with Disabilities.* New York: Aldine De Gruyter, 1987.

Garbarino, J., Guttman, E. and Wilson Seele, J. *The Psychologically Battered Child: Strategies for Identification, Assessment, and Intervention.* San Francisco: Josey-Bass, 1986.

Garbarino, J., Schellenbach, C., Sebes, J. and Associates. *Troubled Youth, Troubled Families.* New York: Aldine, 1986.

Garbarino, James and Gwen Gillian. *Understanding Abusive Families.* Lexington, MA: Lexington Books, 1980.

Gelles, Richard. *Intimate Violence.* New York: Simon and Schuster, 1988.

Gelles, Richard. *Family Violence* (2nd ed.). Newbury Park, CA: Sage Publications, Inc. 1987.

Gil, Eliana and Toni Cavanaugh Johnson. *Sexualized Children.* Rockville, MD: Launch Press, 1993.

Gilbert, N., et al. *Protecting Young Children from Sexual Abuse: Does Preschool Training Work?* Lexington, MA: Lexington Books, 1989.

Halpern, R. "Community-based Early Intervention." In S.J. Meisels and J.P. Shonkoff (eds.), *Handbook of Early Childhood Education.* Cambridge, England: Cambridge University Press, 1990.

Hasslet, Vincent et. al. (eds.). *Handbook of Family Violence.* New York: Plenum Press, 1988.

Hayes, C. ed. *Risking the Future: Adolescent Sexuality, Pregnancy, and Childbearing.* Washington, D.C.: National Research Council, National Academy Press, 1987.

Helfer, R.E. "A Review of the literature on the prevention of child abuse and neglect." *Child Abuse and Neglect,* 6, 1982.

Hendricks, J.E. *Crisis Intervention: Contemporary Issues for On-Site Interveners.* Springfield, IL: Charles C. Thomas, 1985.

Hillman, D. and Solek-Tefft, J. *Spiders and Flies: Help for Parents and Teachers of Sexually Abused Children.* Lexington, MA: Lexington Books, 1988.

Hutchison, Elizabeth D. "Mandatory Report Laws: Child Protective Case Findings Gone Awry?" *Social Work,* Vol. 38, No. 1, January 1993.

Hutchison, E. "Child Maltreatment: Can it be Defined?" *Social Service Review,* 74, 61-78, 1990.

Kadushin, A. and J. Martin. *Child Welfare Services* (4th Ed.). New York: Macmillan, 1988.

Kaminer, B Crowe, A. and Budde-Giltner, L. "The prevalence and characteristics of multidisciplinary teams for child abuse and neglect: a national survey." in D.B. Bross et. al. (eds.). *The New Child Protection Team Handbook.* New York: Garland, 1988.

Kempe, C.H. and Helfer, R. *The Battered Child* (3rd ed.). Chicago: University of Chicago Press, 1980.

Kempe, R. S. and Kempe, C. H. *The Common Secret: Sexual Abuse of Children and Adolescents.* New York: W. H. Freeman, 1984.

Kempe, R. and Kempe, C.H. *Child Abuse.* Cambridge, MA: Harvard University Press, 1978.

Kinsey, A. et. al. *Sexual Behavior of the Human Female.* New York: Pocket Books, 1953.

Knopp, Fay Honey, Freeman-Lange, Bob and William Ferree Stevenson. *Nationwide Survey of Juvenile and Adult Treatment Programs.* Brandon, VT: Safer Society Program & Press, 1992.

Krivacska, J. "Your First Step in Preventing Abuse: Look Critically at Prepackaged Programs." *American School Board Journal,* Vol. 176, No. 4, 1989.

Levine, Carol (ed.). *Programs to Strengthen Families: A Resource Guide.* Chicago, IL: Family Resource Coalition, 1988.

Massachusetts Committee for Children and Youth. *Preventing Child Abuse: A Resource for Policymakers and Advocates.* Boston: Massachusetts Committee for Children and Youth, 1987.

Mayer, A. *Incest: A Treatment Manual for Therapy with Victims, Spouses, and Offenders* (2nd Edition). Holmes Beach, FL: Learning Publications, Inc., 1993.

Mayer, A. *Women Sex Offenders.* Holmes Beach, FL: Learning Publications, Inc., 1991.

Mayer, A. *Sex Offenders: Approaches to Understanding and Management.* Holmes Beach, FL: Learning Publications, Inc. 1988.

Mayer, A. *Sexual Abuse: Causes, Consequences and Treatment of Incestuos and Pedophilic Acts.* Holmes Beach, FL: Learning Publications, Inc., 1985.

McEvoy, A. W. and Brookings, J. *If She Is Raped: A Book for Husbands, Fathers and Male Friends* (2nd ed.). Holmes Beach, FL: Learning Publications, Inc., 1991.

McEvoy, A. *Child abuse law and school policy.* Education and Urban Society 22(3): 247-257, 1990.

McEvoy, A. and Erickson, E. *Youth and Exploitation: A Process Leading to Running Away, Violence, Substance Abuse and Suicide.* Holmes Beach, FL: Learning Publications, Inc., 1990.

McEvoy, M. and McEvoy, A. *Preventing Youth Suicide: A Handbook for Educators and Human Service Professionals.* Holmes Beach, FL: Learning Publications, Inc., 1994.

McEvoy, A. "Abused at home ... besieged at school." *School Intervention Report*, Vol. 2, No. 5, 1989.

McEvoy, Marcia. "Peer assistance programs." *School Intervention Report.* Vol. 3, no. 3, 1990.

Mouzakitis, C.M. and Varghese R. (eds.). *Social Work Treatment with Abused and Neglected Children.* Springfield, IL: C.C. Thomas, 1985.

National Center for Missing and Exploited Children. *Selected State Legislation: A Guide for Effective State Laws to Protect Children* (2nd ed.). Washington, DC: National Center for Missing and Exploited Children, 1989.

National Education Association. *How Schools Can Help Combat Student Pregnancy.* Washington, D.C.: National Education Association, 1988.

Newberger, E. and Bourne, R. *Unhappy Families: Clinical and Research Perspectives on Family Violence.* Littleton, MA: PSG Publishing Co., 1979.

Olsen, L.J. and W.M. Holmes. "Youth at Risk: Adolescents and Maltreatment." *Children and Youth Services Review,* 8:13-35, 1986.

Ovaris, W. *After the Nightmare: The Treatment of Non-Offending Mothers of Sexually Abused Children.* Holmes Beach, FL: Learning Publications, Inc., 1991.

Radbill, Samuel X. "Children in a World of Violence: A History of Child Abuse." Chapter 1 in *The Battered Child* (3rd Ed.), edited by C. Henry Kempe and Ray E. Helfer. Chicago: University of Chicago Press, 1980.

Romano, Casey, K., and D. Daro. *Schools and Child Abuse: A National Survey of Principals' Attitudes, Beliefs, and Practices.* National Committee for Prevention of Child Abuse, Working Paper Number 851, July 1990.

Russell, Diana. *The Secret Trauma: Incest in the Lives of Girls and Women.* New York: Basic Books, 1986.

Russell, D. *Sexual Exploitation.* Beverly Hills, CA: Sage Publications, 1984.

Reitman, A. "Corporal punishment in schools—the ultimate violence." *Children's Legal Rights Journal,* vol 9 no.3, 1988.

Robinson, B. Teenage Fathers. Lexington, MA: Lexington Books, 1988.

Sandberg, David (ed.). *The Child Abuse-Delinquency Connection.* Lexington, MA: Lexington Books, 1989.

Sgori, S. *Handbook of Clinical Intervention in Child Sexual Abuse.* Lexington, MA: Lexington Books, 1982.

"Sibling Abuse." *Virginia Child Protection Newsletter,* Vol. 40, Fall 1993, pp. 1-16.

Stets, Jan E. *Domestic Violence and Control.* New York: Springer-Verlag, 1988.

Straus, Murry and Gelles, Richard. *Physical Violence in American Families.* New Brunswick, NJ: Transaction Publishers, 1990.

Tindall, J. and Gray, H.D. *Peer Counseling: An In-Depth Look at Training Peer Helpers.* Muncie, IN: Accelerated Development, 1989.

Tindall, J. *Peer Power: Applying Peer Helping Skills* (book two). Muncie, IN: Accelerated Development, 1989.

Tower, Cynthia Crosson. *Understanding Child Abuse and Neglect.* Boston: Allyn and Bacon, 1989.

Tower, C.C. *How Schools Can Help Combat Child Abuse and Neglect* (2nd ed.). Washington D.C.: National Education Association, 1987.

Tracy, E., Haapala, D., Kinney, J. and P. Pecora. *Intensive Family Preservation Services: An Instructional Sourcebook.* Cleveland: Case Wester Reserve University Press, 1991.

U.S. Department of Health, Education and Welfare. *Multidisciplinary Teams in Child Abuse and Neglect Programs.* National Center on Child Abuse and Neglect (DHEW), Publication No. (OHDS) 78-30152, August, 1978.

U.S. Advisory Board on Child Abuse and Neglect. *Child Abuse and Neglect: Critical First Steps in Response to a National Emergency.* 1990.

Zabin, L.S. and Hirsch, M.B. Evaluation of Pregnancy Prevention Programs in the School Context. Lexington, MA: Lexington Books, 1988.